ALL I SURVEY

ALL
I SURVEY

A BOOK OF ESSAYS

By

G. K. CHESTERTON

Essay Index Reprint Series

BOOKS FOR LIBRARIES PRESS, INC.
FREEPORT, NEW YORK

First Published 1933
Reprinted 1967

LIBRARY OF CONGRESS CATALOG CARD NUMBER: 67-26723

PRINTED IN THE UNITED STATES OF AMERIC'

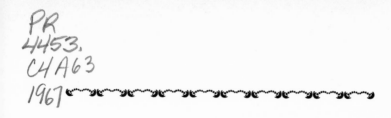

Contents

CONTENTS

ALL I SURVEY

THERE was recently reported in the papers the meeting of certain eminent ladies, of a political and philanthropic sort, who discussed the great modern problem of what is to be done with The Child. I need not say that The Child is always discussed as if he were a monster, of immense size, vast complexity, and strange and startling novelty. Nor need I remind the reader that The Child is not a child: any child we comfortable people have ever seen. The Child is not Jack or Joan or Peter; he is not Cousin Ethel's child or one of Uncle William's children. He is a creature entirely solitary and *sui generis;* and he lives in the slums.

A great many remarks were made, most of them sincere, some of them sensible, and several of them highly comic. I think the passage I like best is one in which a particular female philanthropist said that any poor child would feel happy at the sight of a policeman, so long as he was dressed like a policeman; but that the child might be filled with maniacal terror if he were dressed like an ordinary man. It would seem, that is, that not only are all policemen always kind to all poor people, but that they are the only men who are ever kind to any poor people. I am not The Child, and therefore I was not brought up in the slums. But I know a little more about the slums than that. All these other sayings, however, sink into a second place, in my opinion, compared with one simple remark, which will seem to most people as innocent as it is simple. Nevertheless, in that one artless observation—I might almost say, in that one unconscious confession—was contained the whole complex of contradictions and falsehoods which have in our time ruined the relation of social classes and destroyed the common morals of the community. A very famous political lady, who certainly believes that what she says represents the most lofty luminous idealism, uttered on this occasion the following words: "We must care for other people's children as if they were our own."

And when I read those words, I smote the table with my hand, like one who has suddenly located and smashed a wasp. I said to myself: "That's it! She's got it! She's got the exactly correct formula for the worst and most poisonous of all the political wrongs that rot out the entrails of the world. That is what has wrecked democracy; wrecked domesticity through the breadth and depth of democracy; wrecked dignity as the only prop and pillar of domesticity and democracy. That is what has taken away from the poor man the pride and honour of the father of a household, so that he can no longer really feel any pride or honour in being a citizen; still less in being merely a voter. The Englishman's house is no longer his castle, nor is he king of the castle; the *charbonnier* is no longer *maître chez lui;* his hut is not his hut; his children are not his children; and democracy is dead. She means no harm. She knows not what she does. She does not even understand what she says. She does not comprehend a word of the terrible sentence that she has spoken. But it is spoken." And the sentence that is spoken is this: "We, the rich, can take care of poor people's children as if they were our own. As we have abolished their parents, they are all orphans."

The ideal is sufficiently familiar in fact, of course; and there is nothing very much against it, except that it is utterly and grossly immoral. A man saying that he will treat other people's children as his own is exactly like a man saying that he will treat other people's wives as his own. He may get a certain amount of poetic or sentimental pleasure out of the children, but so he may out of the wives. The question is whether any human rights whatever remain to the other man, who is made legally responsible for his children and his wife. If he ill-treats them, it is perfectly right to put the

exceptional legal machinery, which exists for such exceptional evils, in motion against him. But it is not
right, by any code of common morals yet recognized
among men, to start from the very first with the assumption that his children belong to you as much as they
belong to him. If there is an adequate case against him,
it must be proved against him; but we are not dealing
here with any such case. We are dealing with a profound
plutocratic assumption, accidentally revealed by a chance
phrase. The poor children are born under the power and
protection of a governing class, as wards in Chancery
are born under the power and protection of the Lord
Chancellor; they inherit that status, whether our own
conscience inclines us to call it a status of slavery or of
safety. Note that the lady does not say—though she
doubtless would say—"When I hear of a child being
beaten with a red-hot poker, the common human bond
makes me feel as angry as if it were my own child." She
does not deal with hard cases, or even individual cases;
she generalizes from the start. She assumes that she
will, in fact, manage, she assumes that she will be allowed to manage, any other children as if they were her
own. And in practice she is probably right; it is the
supreme and final proof that in theory she is entirely
wrong. Our society has unconsciously and unresistingly
admitted this great heresy against humanity. The no-

-⟨4⟩-

tion of making the head of a humble family really independent and responsible, like a citizen, has really vanished from the mind of most of the realists of our real world. It is the less wonder that it has never even entered the head of an idealist.

The trouble is that in our society the ideal is more wrong than the real. Old Tories used to insist on teaching to the poor the principles of respect for private property, lest they should revolt and despoil the rich. As a fact, it is the rich who have to be taught about the existence of private property, and especially about the existence of private life. No ragged mob is likely to storm the nurseries of Mayfair, or steal the perambulators from the French nurses, or the pupils from the German governesses, parading in Kensington Gardens. But philanthropists, under various excuses, do really raid the playgrounds of the poor. They regard such a raid as a reform; and, in truth, it is a revolution. Modern writers are very ready to cover great historic events with sweeping denunciations of crime; to say the Great War was murder on a large scale or that the Russian Revolution was theft on a large scale. They hardly realize how much of educational and philanthropic reform has been kidnapping on a large scale. That is, it has shown an increasing disregard for the privacy of the private citizen, considered as a parent. I have called it a revolution;

and at bottom it is really a Bolshevist revolution. For what could be more purely and perfectly Communist than to say that you regard other people's children as if they were your own?

True, as yet the man who treats other people's dogs as if they were his own is called a dog-stealer. The man who is caught, caring for somebody else's horse as if it were his own, is called a horse-thief. But even that is only true if the thieves are poor and too ignorant to plead excuses of humanitarianism. The wealthy Communist who so treats a child is not called a kidnapper. Which only shows that Communism, anyhow *our* Communism, would not be the rule of the poor, nor even the unruliness of the poor; but only the extension of the existing unruliness of the rich.

THIS generation, which is charged with being frivolous, often strikes me as being much too serious. And its culture, which seems in one aspect to verge on anarchy, retains in another aspect a queer weakness for authority. I call it a weakness, because it is not so much an appeal to authority as to authorities. In every scientific or sociological discussion the fact has long been flagrant and farcical. If I mention a piece of elementary common sense, as that, when I find a tooth in Tooting, I am not justified in calling it The Tooting Man, or saying I have "reconstructed" him, I shall certainly get no answer except the stern retort that The Tooting Man was reconstructed by no less a person than Dr. Pidge. If I say (exercising my poor human reason) that to explain Mind as a form of Matter is simply meaningless, like explaining eyes in terms of spectacles, I shall be duly informed that I must give up my poor human reason and accept such mysteries on the authority of Professor Snorter, an authority whose authority is perhaps of greater authority than even all the other authorities. But, while we had grown used to this old joke in the fields of science and philosophy, I cannot but grieve to see it appearing here and there in the milder but more flowery fields of literature and artistic criticism. Doubtless there was a period, in the more remote past, when there was too much weight given in literary criticism to authority and authorities. But one or two recent critics seem to have revived this fault, with a change that makes it even more faulty. If the old critic appealed to writers who were old and forgotten, the new critic thinks it enough to appeal to writers who are new and neglected. But I would just as soon be referred to an antiquity known only to the learned as to a novelty known only to the "cultured." I would rather accept the authority of Aristotle, even at a time when he is known to be unpopular with muddle-headed people, than accept the authority of Mr. Nibbsky, who would be equally unpopular, but is not even known.

I have even found a savour of this spirit in the case of critics better known than Mr. Nibbsky, and better worth knowing. There was a comparatively slight and innocent instance of it in a criticism by Mr. James Agate on a book by Mr. Sidney Dark, writers who have both added to my enjoyment in various ways at various times. The book in question was about Stevenson, who has added to my enjoyment even more. But, as I have only read Mr. Agate's criticism and not Mr. Dark's book,

I will not claim to judge in a general way between them. Only it seems funny to me that the critic should so solemnly make it a condemnation, in itself, of Mr. Dark's book on Stevenson, that it was not piously and reverently founded on Mr. Swinnerton's book on Stevenson. For the critic, apparently, Mr. Swinnerton is the one and only authority on Stevenson, and his sacred name must be invoked, like that of a Muse or a god of inspiration, at the beginning of any literary exercise on the subject. This strikes me as carrying the idolatry of Authority extravagantly far. Mr. Swinnerton is an excellent writer, and doubtless the book in question was an excellent book. But I would still meekly suggest that a man writing on Stevenson should be judged by his appreciation of Stevenson, and not by his appreciation of Swinnerton. But the critic talks with horrible solemnity about "The Pre-Swinnerton" period of Stevensonian criticism. Which really seems to be making too much even of Stevenson, let alone Swinnerton. Men may well be a little mystical in speaking of what is Pre-Adamite, or even Pre-Raphaelite; but I hardly think any of our little text-books of taste and letters will rank with the Renaissance, let alone the Creation.

Of the making of books on Stevenson there is no end; as poor Cranmer observed, "This hath offended; this unworthy hand." But I really doubt whether it was Mr. Dark's moral duty to read all of them before daring to write one of his own. I should as soon think it impertinent of a painter to paint a pine-tree before he had studied all the pine-trees in all the pictures in the world. After all, what we want is direct and individual impressions of primary objects, whether poets or pine-trees, and not an endless succession of critics learning from critics how to criticize. With some parts of Mr. Agate's criticism, whether it be of the book or of the subject of the book, I entirely agree. I should never, for instance, think of resting my real admiration for Stevenson on the slight, and indeed rather thin, essays on the relation of the sexes called *Virginibus Puerisque*. I take them to have been examples of those early exercises in elegant prose, with a preference of manner to matter, to which Stevenson himself humorously confessed in later life. They belong to what is called the "sedulous ape" period, which the yet more sedulous apes of the Press have quoted and requoted sedulously ever since. But Stevenson was not a sedulous ape, any more than Dickens was Boz or Byron was the author of the remarkable poem called "A Tear."

After all, Stevenson died at about the time of life when Dickens had only just written *David Copperfield,* and had not yet attempted so new a departure as *Hard Times* or *Great Expectations;* at an age when any number of great men had still their fullest and most mature work to do. And when he died he was already writing what is quite obviously a much fuller and more mature work, and in many ways quite a new departure. The fragments of *Weir of Hermiston* are like the fragments of a colossal god lying broken in the desert, compared with many of the slender ivory statuettes that he had carved before. But it is an error even to associate him, in his previous work, with things like ivory statuettes. Mr. Huish with his little vitriol-bottle, in *The Ebb-Tide,* would make a very unsuitable ivory statuette. The critic mentioned above falls into this fallacy, I think, when he says that Stevenson "turned all to favour and to prettiness." It is not altogether a fortunate quotation, for it is taken from a scene of grisly tragedy; where the Queen utters it, her voice breaking upon the phrase, when Ophelia wanders half-witted between her lover's murder of her father and her own murder of herself. Many of Stevenson's trifles are quite equally tragic. Many of his pretty phrases accentuate ugly situations. Many of them are not pretty at all. I cannot imagine that any critic rushes to the dreary and bedraggled leavings of *The Ebb-Tide* with a mere childish desire to see the pretty pictures; or that even Mr. Agate would read the account, in *Weir of Hermiston,* of how the oaf, with his neck swathed in flannel, was "hunted gallowswards with jeers," and have merely the sentiments of the infant who kicks his legs and cries: "Oh, pretty, pretty!" These passages strike me as revealing rather too brutal a streak in the writer, due, I think, to the Calvinist pessimism of his original background.

What Stevenson had, and what Stevenson's critics often have not and mistake for mere finesse, was a certain sharpness of *focus*. He did not deal merely with pretty figures, whether they were figures of speech or figures of fiction. On the contrary, he dealt oftener with ugly figures, and certainly enjoyed the ugly figures most. But all the figures are figures, and not merely presences or influences. Mr. Huish is a deformity, but he is a definite form. This may not be the highest artistic quality, but it is not turning everything to prettiness. It is turning everything to beauty, even to the terrible beauty that is made out of a harmony of ugly things. And that is surely not very far off from the primary purpose of art.

OPENING my newspaper the other day, I saw a short but emphatic leaderette entitled "A Relic of Mediævalism." It expressed a profound indignation upon the fact that somewhere or other, in some fairly remote corner of this country, there is a turnpike-gate, with a toll. It insisted that this antiquated tyranny is insupportable, because it is supremely important that our road traffic should go very fast; presumably a little faster than it does. So it described the momentary delay in this place as a relic of mediævalism. I fear the future will look at that sentence, somewhat sadly and a little contemptuously, as a very typical relic of modernism. I mean it will be a melancholy relic of the only period in all human history when people were proud of being modern. For though today is always today and the moment is always modern, we are the only men in all history who fell back upon bragging about the mere fact that today is not yesterday. I fear that some in the future will explain it by saying that we had precious little else to brag about. For, whatever the mediæval faults, they went with one merit. Mediæval people never worried about being mediæval; and modern people do worry horribly about being modern.

To begin with, note the queer, automatic assumption that it must always mean throwing mud at a thing to call it a relic of mediævalism. The modern world contains a good many relics of mediævalism, and most of us would be surprised if the argument were logically enforced even against the things that are commonly called mediæval. We should express some regret if somebody blew up Westminster Abbey, because it is a relic of mediævalism. Doubts would trouble us if the Government burned all existing copies of Dante's *Divine Comedy* and Chaucer's *Canterbury Tales,* because they are quite certainly relics of mediævalism. We could not throw ourselves into unreserved and enthusiastic rejoicing even if the Tower of Giotto were destroyed as a relic of mediævalism. And only just lately, in Oxford and Paris (themselves, alas! relics of mediævalism), there has been a perverse and pedantic revival of the Thomist Philosophy and the logical method of the mediæval Schoolmen. Similarly, curious and restless minds, among the very youngest artists and art critics, have unaccountably gone back even further into the barbaric period than the limit of the Tower of Giotto, and are even now telling us to look back to the austerity of Cimabue and the Byzantine diagrams of the Dark Ages. These relics must be more mediæval even than mediævalism.

But, in fact, this queer phase would not cover only what is commonly called mediævalism. If a relic of mediævalism only means something that has come down to us from mediæval times, such writers would probably be surprised at the size and solidity of the relics. If I told these honest pressmen that the Press is a relic of mediævalism, they would probably prove their love of a cliché by accusing me of a paradox. But it is at least certain that the Printing Press is a relic of mediævalism. It was discovered and established by entirely mediæval men, steeped in mediæval ideas, stuffed with the religion and social spirit of the Middle Ages. There are no more typically mediæval words than those noble words of the eulogy that was pronounced by the great English printer on the great English poet; the words of Caxton upon Chaucer. If I were to say that Parliament is a relic of mediævalism, I should be on even stronger ground; for, while the Press did at least come at the end of the Middle Ages, the Parliaments came much more nearly at the beginning of the Middle Ages. They began, I think, in Spain and the provinces of the Pyrenees; but our own traditional date, connecting them with the revolt of Simon de Montfort, if not strictly accurate, does roughly represent the time. I need not say that half the great educational foundations, not only Oxford and Cambridge, but Glasgow and Paris, are relics of mediævalism. It would seem rather hard on the poor journalistic reformer if he is not allowed to pull down a little turnpike-gate till he has proved his right to pull down all these relics of mediævalism.

Next we have, of course, the very considerable historic doubt about whether the turnpike-gate is a relic of mediævalism. I do not know what was the date of this particular turnpike; but turnpikes and tolls of that description were perhaps most widely present, most practically enforced, or, at least, most generally noted, in the eighteenth century. When Pitt and Dundas, both of them roaring drunk, jumped over a turnpike-gate and were fired at with a blunderbuss, I hope nobody will suggest that those two great politicians were relics of mediævalism. Nobody surely could be more modern than Pitt and Dundas, for one of them was a great financial statesman, depending entirely on the bankers, and the other was a swindler. It is possible, of course, that some such local toll was really mediæval, but I rather doubt whether the journalist even inquired whether it was mediæval. He probably regards everything that happened before the time of Jazz and the Yellow Press as mediæval. For him mediæval only means old, and old only means bad; so that we come to the last question, which ought to have been the first question, of whether a turnpike really is necessarily bad.

If we were really relics of mediævalism—that is, if we had really been taught to think—we should have put that question first, and discussed whether a thing is bad or good before discussing whether it is modern or mediæval. There is no space to discuss it here at length, but a very simple test in the matter may be made. The aim and effect of tolls is simply this: that those who use the roads shall pay for the roads. As it is, the poor people of a district, including those who never stir from their villages, and hardly from their firesides, pay to maintain roads which are ploughed up and torn to pieces by the cars and lorries of rich men and big businesses, coming from London and the distant cities. It is not self-evident that this is a more just arrangement than that by which wayfarers pay to keep up the way, even if that arrangement were a relic of mediævalism.

Lastly, we might well ask, is it indeed so certain that our roads suffer from the slowness of petrol traffic; and that, if we can only make every sort of motor go faster and faster, we shall all be saved at last? That motors are more important than men is doubtless an admitted principle of a truly modern philosophy; nevertheless, it might be well to keep some sort of reasonable ratio between them, and decide exactly how many human beings should be killed by each car in the course of each year. And I fear that a mere policy of the acceleration of traffic may take us beyond the normal modern recognition of murder into something resembling a recognition of massacre. And about this, I for one still have a scruple; which is probably a relic of mediævalism.

WHEN I first heard of the scheme for carving colossal heads of American heroes out of the everlasting hills, the scheme (I think) of the American sculptor, Mr. Borglum, I felt again the thrill first given to me in childhood in reading Nathaniel Hawthorne's fantasy of *The Great Stone Face.* It is not unnatural that two great American artists, in different departments, should have dreamed similar dreams; for the whole conception not only rises out of but really requires the vast American background of prairies and mountain-chains. Anyone will feel, I think, that it would be rather too big for England. It would be rather alarming for the Englishman returning by boat to Dover, to see that Shakspere's Cliff had suddenly turned into Shakspere. We had a distinguished portrait-painter named Beechey, but none of his portraits is quite on the scale of Beachy Head. And the most intrepid mountaineer might well be staggered if, when scaling the steep face of Snowdon, he saw the cold and stony face of Lord Snowden, that far from extinct volcano. Though the heads in the American experiment are those of statesmen, they are mostly those

-{ 19 }-

of statesmen who have passed to where politicians cease from troubling and, at any rate, cease from taxing. But this does not altogether get rid of a further difficulty, even in the more appropriate and spacious American atmosphere.

It is unlucky that at the moment when America can carve permanent historical monuments there has been some loss of permanence in historical theories. America is stronger than any other State just now in certain kinds of architecture and architectural sculpture, suggestive of the stark and starry altitudes of Egypt and Assyria. But the ideas in those ancient designs are either dead or indestructible. In modern history, however, one man has been trying to "debunk" Washington in a book, while another man has been moulding him out of a mountain. What does the "debunker" do in this contest? Does he buy another mountain; and carve another and less pleasing portrait of Washington? Will he prove that the great man was small, by exhibiting his smallness on a large scale? There remains a very fine head of Rameses III, the Pharaoh of the Exodus. But we have not got a colossal caricature of him—by Moses.

That is the mischief with the modern world. We might make more permanent records of our opinions. But we have not got more permanent opinions to record. In every sense we are strong in the concrete; but very wobbly in the abstract. But that is a larger matter than the largest statue, and we cannot conclude upon it here. For my part, I sometimes think public monuments ought to be too large to be seen. I suggest that there should be a new art, plotting out large spaces of the earth in coloured pictures of turf or clay, only to be seen from a skyscraper or a flyingship. Instead of disfiguring the sky with aviators writing advertisements that everybody can see, let us plan out the earth in gigantic figures that only aviators can see. Then anybody who wants to be an æsthete, and talk about Art, can pay a stiff sum to go up to a dizzy and uncomfortable height, and see his own very exclusive portrait gallery spread out before him, over hill and dale, or even over county and province. For things can be kept secret by being large as well as by being small. Hitherto it has been assumed that size and scale in the arts belonged only to things vertical and solid; to architecture or at least to sculpture; and that pictures painted in the flat belong to a world of smaller things, in some cases even concentrating in illuminated missals or in miniatures. By the trifling reform or experiment which I suggest, it would be possible to make pictures more colossal than the most colossal buildings. I will even confess to a weakness for the fancy; there is something faintly stirring to the imagination in the notion of the whole earth traced out in the shapes of

Titans, the earth's huge but forgotten children; or in using the raw colours of geology and the vaster forms of vegetation to fit together into the unity of a sprawling figure or a staring face. It would hardly be safe, of course, to assume that geological areas are plainly coloured like a map; I do not know whether Yellowstone Park is really yellow or the Black Forest really black; in spite of my simple and romantic mind, I am aware that the Red Sea is not red. But, the reds and browns and purples of the desert beside the Red Sea would make excellent material for a certain style of portrait-painting; an admirable if not an enviable complexion. Only, as I say, the æsthete would have to be an aviator, and this alone would probably diminish the number of æsthetes. So that, in a sort of way, I should be a reformer after all. As these vast portraits would be invisible, in a general sense, I suppose it would not matter very much whose portraits they were. But, as a general principle of propriety, I suppose they should only represent men whose names have really gone to the ends of the earth: figures of great national and international power. Meanwhile, the rest of us would never see them and never trouble about them. We should go on living happily and innocently in the woodlands of Abraham Lincoln's whiskers, or in the pleasant shady district not far from the eyebrow of Charles James Fox, without being pestered about Art at all.

It is a fine, large scheme, and more sensible than most large schemes I know. For that would appear to be the logical end of all that pursuit of pure largeness, as such, which has been so much the mark of our time; and has even intoxicated some of the finest intellects of our time, like that of Mr. H. G. Wells. The end of the process of expansion would seem to be disappearance; the vanishing of these vast things from the restricted senses and calculations of man. It is the ultimate upshot of the skyscraper; and upshot seems to be an oddly appropriate term. It is the end that the edifice should tower so high that we cannot see its towers; that the sky-sign should sprawl so wide that we cannot read its lettering; that we should be left, exactly like the people in my parable of the painted earth, living too close to things that are too large. I do not say it is very probable that things will ever go as far as that; chiefly because I think it much more probable that, long before that happens, people will have developed a taste for something totally different; perhaps for things that are microscopically small. But the builders of the big buildings, and the painters of the huge hoardings, do not propose to themselves any logical process except that of making things larger and larger, and therefore have no logical end except to make them too large to bother about.

There is another way in which the parable is really a plain truth; and, indeed, a practical problem. Our relation to modern schemes and systems, to the institutions under which we live and the international influences by which they are extended, is very like the relation of a man living like a pigmy in a city of giants. We have lost the power to control things, largely because we have lost the power to oversee them; that is, to see them as a whole. The economic disasters we suffer are largely due to the operations having grown too large even for the operators. We are all dotted about like little pins stuck in a vast map of financial statesmanship, or rather, financial strategy; it is a plan or chart far too voluminous and bewildering to be at present mastered by any public opinion, and the pins cannot use their pin's-heads. If there are any persons who do understand it, they are much fewer than the aviators who would mount aloft to see the picture of the whole earth.

I HAPPENED recently to renew my acquaintance with Edinburgh Rock; I refer to the remarkable fortress and not the more remarkable foodstuff of that name. The latter, indeed, I am far from despising. There seems even to be something terrible in giving that stark and rugged title to a sweetmeat; as if a child were invited to nibble at Gibraltar or take a big bite out of St. Michael's Mount. Anyhow, that citadel, which is like a city within a city, contains a new and unique building, which is like a castle within a castle. It is the War Memorial of Scotland, and, to my mind, one of the few great War Memorials that are worthy of the greatness of the War. And the train of rambling reflections which it started left me with a profound renewal of all my own original belief in what would now, by comparison, be called little and local things. I have lived through the times when many intelligent and idealistic men hoped that the World War would be an introduction to the World State. But I myself am more convinced than ever that the World War occurred because nations were too big, and not because they were too small. It occurred especially because big nations wished to be bigger, or, in other words, because each State wanted to be the World State. But it occurred, above all, because about things so vast there comes to be something cold and hollow and impersonal. It was *not* merely a war of nations; it was a war of warring Internationalists.

Now, the Scottish War Memorial has a personality. It is the personality of a people, not merely the impersonality of people. I would not raise here, least of all in any unsympathetic spirit, the purely æsthetic debates about the Cenotaph. But, after all, a Cenotaph is by definition an empty tomb, and it affects me individually as a very empty tomb. I would not call it cold and hollow and impersonal in any abusive sense. But it is by its very nature hollow; it is by a deliberate artistic policy impersonal; and the effect of this, on some people at least, is that it is rather cold. The point is that this effect was produced intentionally, and almost inevitably, by the avoidance of anything that could be distinctive of any creed, any province, any profession or branch of the service. It is in that sense cosmopolitan, and therefore colourless; in being the meeting-place of so many races and religions, it can hardly help having something of the hollowness of the heart of the whirlpool, or reminding us of a temple of the winds, offering an intermediate and cold hospitality to all the winds of the world. I know

all that there is to be said for such severities of classic
architecture; but as least those who most admire the
Cenotaph must admire it as architecture, and not as
sculpture. Now, the Edinburgh War Memorial is full of
sculpture, as a mediæval church is full of such carving
and craftsmanship; and the word "full" does really correspond to a sense of fullness. And one effect of that sort
of Gothic fullness is that a thing can be great when it is
small.

Now, a thing like the Cenotaph can hardly be great
when it is small. Even as it is, to my instinct, it is too
small. What I fancy I really feel about it is that it might
be very fine, in its own way, if it were as big as the
Great Pyramid and stood against a background as bare
as the great desert. It might then be entirely artistic and
appropriate, for the artist's own purpose, that it should
be as bare as the sky or as inhuman as the wilderness.
But if we are talking about the human and historical
quality of these things, then there will be surely more
value in a piece of varied and yet concentrated craftsmanship, such as that which has been achieved by this
group of Scottish craftsmen. A carving must be a carving of something, if not of somebody. And the peculiar
liveliness of local life and work lies in the fact that it is
always dealing with something, describing something,
struggling with the particular difficulties of something or

somebody. There is a spirit that can only be called Gossip about a Gothic cathedral and its carvings. It may deal in caricatures, but it does not deal much in those abstract diagrams that can be much more misleading than caricatures. And, without at all narrowing my artistic tastes to this one type or school of work, I will confess to an undiminished partiality for it, because of its extraordinary vitality and vivacity. It is the liveliness of localism, even the liveliness of littleness. It arises when craftsmen have particular positive traditions of the workshop or the shrine, or when there is, for instance, as there still is in Scotland, a living memory of the lineage of particular families, and not only the families of the rich. For no family that is really respected consistently, as a family, can ever be entirely snobbish. The vast voting majority of the very richest family consists of poor relations.

These rambling reflections first began to ramble at the sight of a stone Unicorn, the ancient bearer of the Scottish arms, which stands outside the entrance to the memorial chapel. I thought it was a strong piece of work, simplified, but far from conventional, even in the artistic sense. But what took the eye, as typical of the spirit of which I speak, was the bold but harmonious way in which the artist had dealt with the difficulty of the conventional spike sticking out of the forehead of the sacred monster. The artist had bent the horn back by sheer strength, so to speak—at least by sheer strength of imagination—so that it followed with a wilder curve of its own the strong curve of the horse's neck. And I thought to myself that this was typical of the true spirit of craftsmanship, especially of craftsmanship dealing with definite and traditional symbols. The sculptor had really wrestled with the Unicorn, like a legendary hero wrestling with a fabulous animal. That is, she had really wrestled with a problem of presenting something positive that had to be presented, and yet in a new and more perfect form of presentation. She had made something new out of the old Unicorn; but she had not made anything else except a Unicorn. There was something symbolic in the fact that she had taken that wild, unearthly horse by the horn and forced it back into the contours of her own design. This is only one example out of many, and there are hundreds of such examples, wherever good workmen are doing real work with real images and ideas. Because they are real images and ideas, they can be treated; but they must be treated with. They must be taken on certain terms, and partly on their own terms. Because they are wild things, they can be tamed, but only by the true Unicorn-tamer, who is even more daring than the Lion-tamer.

That is why the traditional art is the truly creative

art. That is why it is truly more creative than the negative abstractions which tend, of their nature, not merely to anarchy, but to nothingness. And that is why a glimpse of these things encouraged me in my own lifelong belief in particularism, and the talés and traditions of a people. Where there are traditions there are tests; where there are traditions there are tasks and practical problems; but they are always stimulants to the spirit and cunning and imagination of man. They are always more fruitful, in the long run, than the work of those who strike outwards to draw a design of nothing on the dark canvas of night. The Unicorn brings forth Unicorns, and all sorts of new and varied Unicorns, and one of them will be different because it is a stone Unicorn and another because it is a bronze Unicorn. But there are no foals born to the Nightmare.

On Old Men Who Make Wars

A STALE and stupid but still poisonous phrase has been buzzing about for the last ten years, as difficult to catch as a wasp in the warm weather. It is already very old, but is always said as if it were something new; everybody has heard it said, and hardly anybody has stopped to ask what it meant. It has many forms, but the commonest form of it is something like this: "Of course the young were embittered when they realized how their elders had brought the world into a horrible catastrophe and a hideous mess." I, for one, am tired of hearing it, and therefore I propose to be the first person who ever thought about it.

First, I happen to remember that exactly the same argument, if you can call it an argument, was used more than twenty years ago, when the fashion was not so much the Appeal to Youth as the Appeal to Woman. Then, also, we were always told that Woman (who had apparently only been born yesterday) looked around her and saw a world of sin and sorrow. This, she promptly declared, was a Man-Made World. Her supporters were not content to say that she was unjustly treated, as in many ways she was; they were not content to say that she had as much claim as man to this or that legal or social privilege: which was very arguable, and about which, in any case, I am not now going to argue. They did definitely declare that the wickedness and misery of the world were clearly due to the fact that it had been managed by males. If the wasp came in at the window and stung somebody, this was due to the fact that it was a Man-Made window, if not actually a Man-Made wasp. If Woman had been in control of the world, there would have been no wasps; or all the wasps would have been trained in such tact and social discipline that they never stung anybody. If the poor were underpaid or overworked, it was solely because men and not women had the paying of them, though some of us had known women who were hard on their subordinates, almost in the manner of men. If nations went to war, it was because women had not votes to stop them, though some of us knew women who waved flags and shouted war-songs and were far more passionately patriotic than the males whom they sent to war. Whatever evil there was on the earth, it was due to the fact that humanity, for reasons best known to itself, had given all power to the sex that always supported evil, and no power at all to the sex which invariably, and in every situation, supported the highest possible good.

I remember all that sort of talk, that started nearly thirty years ago, and attributed all misfortunes to Men. I still hear the other sort of talk, that started nearly twenty years ago, and attributes all misfortunes to Old Men.

Since then, the first batch of Young Men have themselves almost become Old Men; but they are still saying it. They are still saying it without seriously thinking about it. Anyone who will examine the statement will see that it really rests on three assumptions which, as is usual in these cases, are not only accepted, but accepted unconsciously. The speakers not only assume them without proving them, but assume them without knowing they are assuming them. The first is this: That terrible and desolating tragedy is so abnormal in human life, and so utterly out of the nature of things, that it can only be attributed to the staggering and scandalous stupidity of some special individual or individuals. Without going off into an argument about human life, we may note that there is at least an element which is here ignored for the first time in history; for that tragic character of living was a commonplace to all the sages and the poets. To put it shortly, if it is terrible that two million men should die together in a campaign, it is also terrible that all men without exception must die separately somewhere. It is not self-evident that the tragic phase of life only follows on exceptional folly, and the fallacy was noted some time ago by the Tower of Siloam and the Ash-heap of Job.

The second assumption is this: That a tragedy like the Great War must have been not only a blunder, but a blunder made by everybody at the same moment. It must have been a blind collision in the dark, and therefore can only have been due to mere negligence in all those in control. Now you may or may not agree that there was an aggressor in the quarrel, but it is nonsense to assume it as self-evident that there was not, or talk as if there could not be. If there was, the affair would not be a result of negligence, but emphatically a result of vigilance. We may say it was a wicked vigilance on the part of the aggressor; but, by the same stroke, we are forced to admit that it was therefore a just and honour-able vigilance on the part of the defenders. Anyhow, the whole nightmare of mere negligence has disappeared as a necessity of logic; it has disappeared because it was not a necessity but a mere assumption.

Thirdly (though this point is less easy to limit and define properly): It is an assumption to suppose that statesmen or national leaders *are* necessarily wrong even when they do risk great catastrophes, for the sake of creating or preserving some cultural system associated with all that makes life worth living. A man might admit that his efforts to aver catastrophe might fail, that the catastrophe might follow, and still maintain his course, being resolved at least to avoid the worst catastrophe of the loss of the main hope of humanity. Certainly every reform or reconstruction in human history has been followed by calamities, if wars are the chief calamities. The democratic ideal of Athens involved it in a welter of wars; the universal civilization of Rome was spread by a long routine of wars; every national culture owes something to the national wars. If you accept the French Revolution, it covered Europe with the Napoleonic Wars. If you accept the Protestant Reformation, it devastated the Germanies with the longest and weariest of all wars. If you accept the Russian Revolution, it has already produced endless internal wars, one external war, and the end is not yet. I am not expressing admiration for war, nor, for that matter, for the Russian Revolution or the Reformation. I am only saying that nobody has a right to assume at the start that no statesman has any right to risk war, for the sake of ideals that change or preserve civilization. In short, there was nothing grotesquely doddering and decadent about the Old Men who, twenty years ago, tried to rule the troubled and troublesome race of men. Some were right and some were wrong; but most were vigilant, and all were bound in any case to take a risk.

I think this worth mentioning now, for a simple reason. We are already drifting horribly near to a New War, which will probably start on the Polish Border. The Young Men have had nineteen years in which to learn how to avoid it. I wonder whether they do know much more about how to avoid it than the despised and drivelling Old Men of 1914. How many of the Young Men, for instance, have made the smallest attempt to understand Poland? How many would have anything to say to Hitler, to dissuade him from setting all Christendom aflame by a raid on Poland? Or have the Young Men been thinking of *nothing* since 1914 except the senile depravity of the Old Men of that date?

M. PAUL CLAUDEL's play, *The Satin Slipper*, translated
with admirable subtlety and flexibility by the Rev. John
O'Connor, is a work of rich and almost bewildering
fantasy, and has any number of aspects that could not
adequately be treated here. But it has one particular
aspect, in which it is related to recent events in other
fields, and rather specially calls for a particular comment just now. Though nobody could be more French
than M. Claudel, and nothing could be more French
than the particular kind of wit and fighting logic that
pursues this theme or thesis to its end, yet the whole
background of the drama is the background of the
Spanish civilization. Even at this moment the Spanish
civilization is something very much larger than the
civilization of Spain. It was infinitely more so in the
days of the external glory of Spain, the days of the
alliance with Austria and the conquest of America.
About all that culture there was a character which runs
through this drama like a decorative pattern, and will
be found more and more, I think, to be a pattern for
the art of today.

-ᘓ37ᘒ-

Thus, no two poets could possibly be more different in every tradition or test of historical type than Paul Claudel and Vachel Lindsay, the spirited American singer. In external and formal attachment, they would seem utterly foreign to each other. Vachel Lindsay was a Puritan in the personal sense; one might almost say in the political sense. He was even a Prohibitionist, and it is only fair to say that his orgiastic verse does demonstrate how very drunk a man can be without wine when he drinks the American air. Occasionally, even, a critic might be tempted to call it the American hot-air. For though Vachel Lindsay was a natural artist, and went right by the clue of the imagination, there are passages of his finest writing which would have been finer still if he had not lived in the land of the megaphone rather than the ivory horn; or if his traditions had not given him the choice of two trumpets—the brazen trumpet of publicity as well as the golden trumpet of poetry. He was himself a wholly simple, sincere, and therefore humble man; but the people around him did not believe in humility; no, not even when they practised it. But they did believe in go and gusto and the big noise; and to a certain extent Vachel Lindsay even at his best did practise that. I have myself a huge sympathy with his special gift for describing men banging their gongs to the glory of their gods; but it were vain to deny that in some ways their gods were not our gods. Most certainly, anyhow, they were not M. Claudel's gods. M. Claudel is not only a Catholic, but a French Catholic; with the particular French dislike of orgiastic religion and the fads that invade domesticity. I should imagine that there are no two things that M. Claudel would be more completely puzzled to comprehend than (1) a free man being a Prohibitionist, and (2) a fine poet selecting from all human history the subject of "General Booth Enters Heaven."

And yet both poets, the Frenchman and the American, illustrate this third element that is neither American nor French. For truly Vachel Lindsay was something more than an American; he was (wildly as the term would be misunderstood) a Spanish-American. He was, spiritually speaking, a Californian. He did not get drunk only on the American air; he drank the air of a strange paradise, which is in some way set apart and unlike anything in the New World or the Old; a fairy sea, calmed as by a spell, that stretches far away into fantastical China and of which even the nearer coast is ruled by ghosts rather than by its modern rulers. For there is spread all along that Pacific Coast, in some fashion too vivid for definition, the presence and the pressure and the splendour of Spain. It was something in this rich sunset air that got into the verse of a Puritan like Vachel Lindsay, and made it so much more instinctively ornate and gorgeous than that of a mere Pagan like Walt Whitman. Whitman was a great man; but he was a man of the Eastern States and of the Northern sun, and therefore his passion was colourless even when it was not cold. The Puritanism of Lindsay was more glowing than the Paganism of Whitman. And the reason was, I think, this unconscious influence which possesses all the West of America, as the old Celtic romance possesses all the West of England. The poetry of Vachel Lindsay proves, in every sort of broken and unconscious fashion, how much he was haunted by this presence; how much he felt under his feet this Spanish subsoil of American States. It was, to quote the words of his own vision, the Wrecks of the Galleons of Spain that towered and swelled above him in a sort of glowing monstrosity, and gave their real symbolic outline to the Golden Whales of California.

In other words, it is worth while to realize that there is spread over great spaces of the earth a sort of Spanish magic. The Spanish settlements are not what is called dead-alive places, in the sense of places in which the living are dead; they are places in which the dead are alive. But the dead are alive, even where nobody else is alive. Even the deserted parts of that coast are not a desert; and even the dead parts of that empire cannot die. And it is the vast vitality of that dead empire that attracts a French northerner like M. Claudel, just as it unconsciously attracted an American like Mr. Lindsay. The dramatic narrative of M. Claudel, as I have said, covers a vast field of universal ideas and individual problems. It is full of what is found in the very name of The Golden Whales of California, and it is a whale of a book. But it is also golden, in the sense of being full of things that are truly as good as gold. It even rather excels in the description of things shapeless or of incalculable shape, like such gigantic monsters; indeed, as it happens, there is a typically grotesque description of the actual animals called whales. "Their head, which is like a whole mountain full of liquid sperm, shows in the corner of the jaw a little eye no bigger than a waistcoat-button." There is the same sort of imaginative sense of the shape of something shapeless in this fine phrase about the amorphous Germanies of Central Europe. "To know it you must look at its heart, for it has got no face."

All that dark and yet exuberant imagery belongs to a tradition that can be seen in the art and ornament of Spain. It can be seen in the special Spanish love of black; the black which is not the negation of colour, but rather the accumulation of colour. It can be seen in the rich darkness of Spanish churches, fretted with the golden fire of countless candles. But it can be seen fully and completely only in the world-wide spreading of the Spanish culture in the sixteenth century, when it met on its borders monsters stranger than whales; red men and golden mountains and a new world. It had many crimes, which are not hidden in Claudel's poem, but it had this very enviable greatness: that strange stars and new sciences were then opened to a Christian world that was still full of chivalry. Then wicked men colonized for greed, but good men did not colonize only for commerce; when the white man was as romantic a figure as the red man, and trade had not destroyed the Red Indian to replace him by the Regular Guy.

IT is an eternal truth that the fathers stone the prophets and the sons build their sepulchres; often out of the same stones. For the reasons originally given for execution are often the same as the reasons given later for canonization. But it might be added that there is often a third phase, in which the grandsons wreck and reduce to ruins the sepulchres that the sons have made. The process of the acceptation or rejection of prophets, true and false, is not quite so simple a progress as it appeared to the progressive philosophy of the nineteenth century. It is full of ups and downs; even for a dead prophet, who is not generally allowed to remain dead in peace. And nothing is more curious than to note the way in which this change does affect great reputations, and especially revolutionary reputations.

The curious thing is that, when the rebellion comes, it is generally a rebellion against rebels. It is generally *not* a rebellion against reactionaries. Men in the past who particularly praised the past may in some cases have faded into the past which they praised. But they have not often been singled out for special attack by the future which they despised. Those who were, in fact, doomed to dethronement in the future were generally the futurists of the past. It was those who were promising men a future of greater glory, who had really before themselves a future of greater discredit and neglect. The old dusty and musty *laudator temporis acti* may sometimes be neglected, but he is seldom discredited. He is never dethroned, possibly because he has never been enthroned. But he seems to outlast any number of the enthroned prophets of progress.

I am noting this as a singular historical fact, quite apart from my own sympathies, which are sometimes with the revolutionary and sometimes with the reactionary. For instance: suppose a man were asked which were the two greatest Englishmen, or rather the two greatest British subjects, alive at the end of the eighteenth century. Opinions might differ; but a man would not be very far wrong if he said Byron and Burke. At that time Burke stood, as he stands in all his most important work, as the champion of Conservative ideas; the man who urged us to preserve even irrational traditions; the man who lamented over the loss of even older traditions. He was then emphatically the Burke who lamented aloud that the age of chivalry was past, or wept over the vanished beauty of the French Queen. On the other hand, Byron was at that time emphatically the voice of the Revolution. He openly regretted that it had been defeated at Waterloo; he lashed all the Tories with a scourge of satire, which he flourished like a flag of Liberty. Well, they were both great men, and, if I have a purely personal preference, it is for Byron. It is certainly, in most respects, for the political party of Byron. And yet it cannot be denied that the subsequent relations of the two reputations, to fame or at least to fashion, have illustrated this curious advantage of the reactionary over the revolutionary. Byron has been, I think rather underrated ever since. Burke has been, I think, rather overrated ever since. That is a matter of opinion; but it is a matter of fact that Burke has not been very specially denounced or derided, whereas Byron has been incessantly denounced and derided. It came to be almost the mark of a modern and advanced intellectual to be always sniffing and sneering at the mere rhetoric and melodramatic romance of Byron. Nobody specially insisted that Burke's rhapsodies about Marie Antoinette were mere rhetoric, as they undoubtedly were. Certainly there is something, which it were mild to call melodrama, in saying about that hearty German lady: "And surely never lighted upon this orb, which she scarcely seemed to touch, a more delightful vision." That florid phraseology is not allowed to return to the mind when Mr. Buckle or Mr. Garvin are describing

the debt of our Constitution to the subtle and states-
manlike philosophy of Burke. Burke never became a sort
of cockshy for the critics, and Byron did. And it does
seen rather to suggest that, if you are a prophet of resur-
rection and revolution, of the future and of the dawn,
your sepulchre is likely to be pelted and defaced even
after it has been built. But if you were only a builder of
sepulchres, your sepulchre will be left in peace.

Then consider the next and still more singular stage
in the story. The whole story was repeated over again,
towards the end of the Victorian era, when Swinburne
arose to dispute the mild constitutional monarchy of
Tennyson and in some sense to fill once more the revolutionary throne of Byron. The first thing to notice is
that there is no sympathy, certainly no continuity, between the old rebel and the new rebel. Swinburne was
just as ready to dismiss or despise Byron as all the other
people of his æsthetic time and school, or rather readier
than the rest. There was no sympathy between revolution
and revolution, simply because there was no sympathy
between fashion and fashion. "Farewell, ye gay something, ye gardens of roses" (I regret to say that I forget
what the gay something was) sounded at once florid
and frigid to a generation which did not feel that "If
love were what the rose is, and I were like the leaf,"
might be not only unnatural, but very nearly non-

sensical. Every novelty has its own nonsense, and never sees that it is nonsense, and always sees that the older novelty was nonsense. But Swinburne himself is already becoming an older novelty, and there are any number of people who are beginning to say that his poetry is nonsense. It seems highly probable that he, in his turn, is in for a period of reaction and ridicule; in which his work will be underrated exactly as Byron's was under-rated. But he will be underrated for the same reason—simply because he was overrated; but, above all, because he was especially overrated as a rebel and a reformer and a new force making for the future. The man who sits down to compose *Songs Before Sunrise* is apt to find the sun, when it rises, rather too hot for him.

But the point is that what seems to attract this strange revolt is not being an ancient king, but being an ancient rebel. The world swung back on Byron in proportion to the strength with which he had swayed it as a fashion-able demagogue; and the same thing that happened to Byron is now obviously happening to Swinburne. It is not so obviously happening to those of Swineburne's contemporaries, who, though they shared the artistic methods of the time, were really interested in the artistic models of an earlier time. I have mentioned the only too-recurrent subject of roses. I have noted how remote were the full-blown rose-gardens of Byron from the "mystical rose of the mire" so much celebrated by Swinburne. I fear it is only too likely that, in the anti-Swinburnian reaction, a great many people will make fun of shamelessly alliterative lines like "The raptures and roses of vice," which certainly does not mean very much. But I doubt if they will trouble to make game of William Morris's line, "Two red roses across the moon," though it means absolutely nothing at all. But then Morris, in spite of his revolutionary side, was saved by his reactionary side. He was really more interested in the past than in the future, so the future may leave him alone.

I could give a great many other instances of how the Pagans of yesterday are being mocked by the Pagans of today. A man speaking of fine English prose in my boyhood would probably have mentioned both Pater and Newman. I have lately heard an amazing number of people sneering at Pater; I have not heard many people, or indeed any people, sneering at Newman. Yet it would certainly have been said that the Pagan looked to the future and the Papist to the past. I draw no moral from this curious habit of humanity. I am content to be, for once, an utterly unmoral critic of the Swinburne period, or a cold, rationalist scientist of the Victorian Age.

IX   *On Dependence and Independence*

I CAME across a lady quite lately who leapt up in a flame of noble indignation at the suggestion that her husband should pay for her dresses, though she did not apparently object to his paying for her dinners. I admit that there was something fine and generous about such perversity, and that she was an improvement on other ladies who leap up in a flame of indignation because their husbands will *not* pay for a hundred dresses a month. It is sometimes the husband who leaps up in a flame of indignation, and in neither case is the indignation so noble. All the same, it seems to me an instance of the queer welter of inconsequent and inconclusive notions that make it so difficult for the modern world to establish a normal social rule.

Some of us (who cannot be called conservative in the sense of content with social conditions, and who have even been called revolutionary for our attempts to improve those conditions) have nevertheless come to have a profound suspicion of what is called Progress. And the reason is this: that there does not seem to be a principle, but only principles, and these conflicting principles, of Progress. There is not a stream, but a sort of eddy or whirlpool. There could not be a stronger case than this particular ideal of Independence. It is not made the principle of social reform. Even the social reformers would be the first to say that they depend on dependence; on the mutual dependence of comrades and fellow-citizens, as distinct from the individualistic independence they would denounce as mere isolation. It is not made the ideal of the proletarian or wage-earner, either by the Communist or the Capitalist system. Both the Communist and the Capitalist are alike in *not* thinking of the individual worker as independent. They will discuss whether he is well paid, whether he is well treated, whether he works under good or bad conditions, whether he is dependent on a good or bad business or a good or bad government; but *not* whether he is independent. Independence is not made the ideal of the normal man. It is only suddenly and abruptly introduced, in one particular relation, in the case of the exceptional woman. She is only independent of her husband; not independent in any other real relation of life. She is only independent of the home—and not of the workshop or the world. And it is supremely characteristic of this confusion that one well-meaning individual should make a yet finer distinction, and resolve to be independent in the dressing-room, but not in the dining-room.

Now, the modern trouble is that moral scraps and fragments of this sort are floating about like icebergs, and nobody knows when he will bump into one of them. In one case somebody will make an excuse of the ideal of Service, even if it means servility. In another case somebody will make an excuse of the ideal of Individuality, even if it means insanity. People will make attempts at despotism, or demands for freedom, successively or even simultaneously, according to a quite arbitrary program of opportunism. And we feel that they are not submitting a variety of actions to one test; they are applying a variety of tests to one action, which is for them already a fixed and settled action. They do what they want, and make up reasons for it afterwards; but even the reasons are rather too cunning to be reasonable. In a word, it is this chaos, in the creed and code of conduct, that prevents a man from finding in it any sort of guide, even a guide to progress. Thus, in the present case, we could at least settle down to discussing seriously the Independence of Woman, if it were regarded by anybody as part of a real philosophy of the Independence of Man. What we find, as in the case mentioned, is that one woman has made one claim to one curious and rather capricious form of independence. She is independent of the breadwinner, but not of the bank or the employer—not to mention the moneylender.

Thus, to begin with, it would be well to note what economic independence means: as distinct, that is, from what it ought to mean. It might mean that the lady went out into a primeval forest to slay lions and leopards and clothe herself with their skins, like Diana. It might mean that she sewed together the leaves of the forest and made herself a green garment, like Eve. It might mean that she held herself independent in owning her own spinning-wheel and her own store of thread, and weaving strips of simple drapery, like Mr. Gandhi. In a word, she might be really independent of the dress allowance, in the sense of being independent of the dressmaker. It is not very likely that it does mean this; but it is not the dependence on the dressmaker that is the serious inconsistency in the idea. It is the fact that modern woman, in the condition of modern society, will herself have to work, if not for a dressmaker, then probably for somebody else who is primarily the money-maker. And the question is, why is it any better to be a proletarian in the shop than to be a Communist in the home? For the only truly and legitimately Communist institution is the home. "With all my worldly goods I thee endow" is the only satisfactory Bolshevist proclamation that has ever been made about property. It is, therefore, of course, the one proclamation which Bolshevists would be the first to attack. The twisted and

unnatural posture of the modern controversy, like that
of a serpent with its tail in its mouth, biting and tearing
at itself, is excellently illustrated in this queer revolt of
Communism in the wrong place against Communism
in the right place. We no longer make the normal attempt to break up society into homes. We only make
an attempt to break up homes, and even that by a
principle of division which we dare not apply to anything else in society. The crack or fissure is to run across
the hearth or the roof-tree, but to be concealed as far as
possible from the forum or the street.

We hear a great deal of the evil passions of Class War
and the suggestion that the master and man must of
necessity be natural enemies. But surely there is a far
more perverse implication pervading the modern world;
that the wife and the husband are natural enemies. They
are, apparently, such mortal enemies that it is enough
for one of them to be freed from the other, even in one
trumpery particular, though she is not freed from anything or anybody else. The whole of the rest of the
world in which she lives, whether for good or evil, is
one network of necessitarian dependence. People have
left off even talking the language of independence; the
old language about the thrift that leads to independence
or the self-respect that comes from independence. Anybody may find himself almost abjectly dependent upon

anybody; any woman may do the same. And apparently it does not matter, so long as it is not her own husband and not concerned with her own hats. I should very much like to see some of these good-natured groping people draw up something like a plan or table of their real conception of a social structure, and of the necessary commandments of society. The newspapers talk about the danger of Bolshevism, and the Red Peril. But I am afraid of the Patchwork Peril, which is all colours and none; I am afraid of bits of Bolshevism and bits of insane individualism and bits of independence in the wrong place, floating hither and thither and colliding with they know not what; the icebergs whose very shapelessness, or incalculable shape, has always been the cause of shipwreck.

EVERYBODY knows, or ought to know, that making a universal theory about human society is the easiest thing in the world. The reason is not always so apparent, but I think there is a reason which can be stated rationally. The logical weakness in this sort of superficial social theory is this: that the social values are not fixed like mathematical values, and can themselves be moulded to fit the theory. If I say that red-haired men are always the tallest men in the world, I can probably be very rapidly refuted; because measuring men with a six-foot rule is a matter of mathematical fact. But if I say that red-haired men are always the men who sway the destinies of the world, I can always make out a case, by taking all the red-haired men who were important and making them out more important than they were. I can invent an ingenious theory that it was William Rufus rather than William the Conqueror who really confirmed the Norman monarchy which became the English nation. I shall have an easier task in showing that Henry the Second, the first Plantagenet, really was a great man who in some sense ruled a great empire. I can argue that

General James Wolfe, who (I believe) had red hair, was the greatest of England's heroes, by arguing that Canada is really the greatest of England's possessions. I can say that the only man who really influenced the intellectual life of our time was Bernard Shaw. I might make out quite a good case; but my motive is merely in the fact that Mr. Shaw had a red beard not so very long ago; though presumably he has grown less wise as he has grown more white. But the point is that I must maintain the general proposition of his wisdom; and I may find myself committed to defending a large number of rather extraordinary propositions, normally remote from my own mental habits; not through a dis- interested conviction that Mr. Shaw is wise as well as witty, but because I am committed to a general dogma that the red-haired man is always right.

It will be well illustrated in the case of Queen Elizabeth, a topic almost as controversial as Bernard Shaw. For the sake of my theory, I must cling desper- ately to the old-fashioned view that I was taught at school; the theory that the red-haired Queen Bess was a sort of tawny lioness of royal magnanimity and heroic religious convictions, shaking the earth with her roar- ings on behalf of the Reformation. I must not listen to the later and more realistic historians, who tell us that Elizabeth was personally an invalid and politically very much of a tool; that her real religious attachments are very doubtful, and her external political actions mostly forced on her by Cecil and his gang. In the ordinary way, I might be quite indifferent, and therefore quite impartial. But I must fight to the death for the old theory of the Froude and Freeman period; not so much for the cause of the lady as for the colour of her hair. I need her for my general plan of painting the map red; or, rather, of tying it up in red hair instead of red tape. This is how it happens that perverse and pedantic fancies so often harden into fanaticism among professors and professional historians. They will maintain any paradox rather than lose any point that supports their pet generalization, even if they do not personally care very much about the point itself. There was a mediæval tradition that Judas had red hair; and this sort of don would not shrink from saying that Judas and not Jesus was the real founder of Christianity.

I may seem to dwell on an arbitrary and absurd example. But it is not so. I myself grew up under the gigantic shadow of the Teutonic Theory. It was essentially a theory that everything valuable had been done by fair-haired men, which is quite as ludicrous as the same assertion about red-haired men. But I am not now interested in attacking that theory, or any other theory. I only remark that such theories, whether true or false, do affect the truthfulness of historians, and more often in the direction of falsehood than of truth. When we find professors quibbling and quarrelling about the number of men living on a farm mentioned in Dooms-day Book, or the terms of a dispatch sent to a French marshal before the Battle of Arcola, we may be pretty certain that, though these are the things about which they are quibbling, they are not the things about which they are quarrelling. There lies behind some much larger quarrel about some much larger theory; probably some theory about the religion of the Middle Ages or the motives of the French Revolution. History and sociology can never be "scientific" in the sense of subject to exact measurement, because there is always the mystery and doubt inherent in moral evidence affecting one half of the equation, and generally both. In the thesis that red-haired men are great men, there are shades of difference even in red hair, and infinite shades of difference in greatness or the pretence of greatness. And not a few modern theorists seem to me to be strangely lacking in the instinct of what is really great.

It is amusing to notice how these theories pursue each other, and how the last almost always devours and de-stroys the last but one. Generally, in fact, the last is the flat contradiction of the last but one. Generally they are equally extreme, equally exaggerated, and, so far, equally untrue. For instance, the general theory implied in a book like *The Outline of History* is that the outline is a continuous and ascending line, a single upward curve with very few breaks in it. I do not mean that the author denies decay and reaction, but that the main moral he would like to draw is that the host of humanity has advanced, with a few halts, along the high road of history. Above all, he implies a human unity, and the idea that the host that has halted is the same as the host that has advanced. I think myself that he greatly exaggerates this continuity; leans too heavily on the alleged links, and especially misses the missing links. He makes the amoeba and the anthropoid much nearer to us than they really are. At the same time, he makes the ancient Greek or the mediæval Christian much more inferior to us than they really are. He makes the progress too recent, too rapid, and too clear. For instance, he assumes that the mediæval idea of education was inferior to ours, simply because it involved the teaching of a positive philosophy. But there is something to be said for the idea of teaching everything to somebody, as compared with the modern notion of teaching nothing, and the same sort of nothing, to everybody. For what we force on all families, by the power of the police, is not a philosophy but the art of reading and writing unphilosophically. I am not, however, contesting the world-theory of Mr. Wells at this moment. I am only contrasting the world-theory of Mr. Wells with the world-theory which instantly followed it across the world.

For the next thing we heard was that all Europe and America were full of a new fuss made about the general theory of a German writer, whose whole point was that human history was *not* continuous, and *not* progressive, and *not* a thing presenting points of comparison between one stage and another. According to this new theory, there is only a series of closed cycles of different cultures, so separate that they can hardly be compared. We may say that there is no progress, but only progresses. We might almost say that there is no history, but only histories. When the Greek and Roman culture commonly called Antiquity had ended, it broke off without any bridge connecting it with the mediæval or the modern. It is the fossil of a lost world, and no more of a lesson to us than a pterodactyl to a bird-fancier or Eohippus to a horse-breeder. Now, this also is certainly a gross exaggeration. There is a great deal more continuity, and in that sense a great deal more progress, than is allowed for in that historical theory. For instance, nobody understands the Middle Ages without realizing that the mind of Aristotle was still labouring in its midst like a mighty mill; and it is absurd to say that Augustine and Aquinas were not parts of the same continuous communion. But what interests me is not the truth or falsehood of the first or second theory. It is that they so flatly contradict each other, and that they so rapidly followed each other. And I fall back on my first reflection: that theories of that sort must be rather easy to make up—if you leave out more than half the facts.

THERE is still a fashion of making fun of the Victorians as very solemn people, but on that point I rather fancy they are still making fun of us. I am very far from being a mere apologist for Victorianism. But it seems to me that in many ways it is they who were frivolous and their descendants who are serious; quite unduly serious. For instance, what is hailed as a new style or a new school in literature often consists of doing as a novelty what a Victorian did long ago as a joke. Thus we have, in Mr. James Joyce or Miss Gertrude Stein, the coining of new words by the confusion of old words; the running of words together so as to suggest some muddle in the subconsciousness. I do not recall the particular examples, but they would think nothing of saying that somebody was "drurgling," meaning "gurgling when drunk," or that somebody else was "widaslepe," meaning that he had fallen asleep at the moment of saying he was wide awake. I do not doubt that they really do this much more cleverly than I can imitate it. In expressing confused ideas, the moderns have great subtlety and sympathy. It is in expressing clear ideas that they generally find their limitations. All that concerns me here is that this literary style is offered to us, with unimpeachable solemnity, as a rebirth of language or a new power in the mind of man.

Now, Lewis Carroll was a very Victorian Victorian. But he did identically the same thing; only he happened to know that it was funny, and therefore he did it for fun. He invented what he called "portmanteau words," with the sense of two words telescoped into one. Thus he explained that "brillig" is a combination of "brilliant" and "grilling"; or that "slithy" is a portmanteau of "lithe" and "slimy." This particular instance happens to illustrate what I mean when I say that I am not a mere partisan. The author of *Alice in Wonderland* is not an ideal being whom I revere, or hold up to be revered. In some respects he was much too Victorian a Victorian. On some matters he really was much too solemn. But he was not solemn about portmanteau words; and the admirers of Miss Stein are quite solemn about them. On an all-round view of cultural traditions and spiritual potentialities, I think it probable that I should very much prefer Mr. Joyce to Mr. Dodgson. But there is no getting over the historical fact that the Victorians could, in fact, invent these fancies, and could enjoy them for the fun of the thing. Whereas, in the general view of life suggested by the later schools, there is no fun and precious little enjoyment.

Over and above the light nonsense of the nineteenth century, which anticipated so much of the heavy nonsense of the twentieth, it is curious to note that the whole record is hardly encouraging to the more solemn sort of experiments. For the Victorian Age also had its experiments. The Victorian Age also contained men of letters, and even men of genius, who wrote in new styles regarded as uncommon, ugly, obscure, *outré*, or over-subtle. And the extraordinary thing is that it is exactly those writers who have faded out of fashion and favour. There is much less intellectual excitement than there used to be about Browning. There is a quite startling silence and indifference about Meredith. Here again I am in no sense dealing with my own preferences, or discussing whether I regret or rejoice in these changes. It so happens that I always have been, and still am, very fond of Browning's work. It so happens that I never did become a pure and perfect Meredithian in the appreciation of Meredith's work. But I am talking about the facts of fashion and appreciation. And I confess I think it much more likely that there will be a rapid revival of Tennyson than a rapid revival of Browning. I know, as everybody knows, that there is a sort of worship (I am tempted to say a sort of idolatry) of the comparatively straightforward novels of Hardy, and something rather like a negative iconoclasm following the select idolatry once dedicated to Meredith. I do not know why this is so; I do not especially rejoice that it is so; I rather prefer the pantheism of Meredith to the pessimism of Hardy. But it does suggest that there is a mistake somewhere in the current theory that the eccentric of one age is the centre of the next. Browning has not left a dynasty of Browning's writing in Browningese. Meredith has not left a new literature, full of the typical fancies and freedoms, twists and turns, of the true Meredithian dialect. There is a moral to the Victorian Age, and it is a lesson of something to avoid. But it is rather a warning against being unconventional than merely against being conventional. We have many odd writers, writing in odd styles, in our own time; and they may or may not retain influence in later times. But I cannot remember a single Victorian with an odd style whose odd style is now of any advantage to him: not Carlyle; not Browning; not Meredith; not Doughty. The one solitary exception I remember, whose name has somewhat floated to the surface again of late, is that of Gerard Hopkins.

Thus I have a purely intellectual doubt of the future of fads, and even of fancies, unless they are treated frankly in a fanciful manner. I do not think any such experiment succeeds in twisting the tradition of language out of its common tendency. I can easily believe that a book like *Ulysses* is a striking and original book in its place and time; like *Sartor Resartus* in its place and time. But I do not believe that Mr. Joyce has added a new range or direction to literary expression, any more than Carlyle succeeded in turning the English language into a bastard barbaric version of the German language. I can easily suppose that Miss Stein likes having her little joke, especially at the expense of the reader; just as George Meredith certainly liked having his little joke at the expense of the reader. But the fact remains that, at the present moment, the trouble is not that the reader does not understand him, but that the reader does not read him. I grieve to say, from what I know of human nature and history, that I doubt whether posterity will even try to understand Miss Stein. So that she will share her little joke with her Creator until the end; which may be quite a good joke too. But the theory that has been so common of late, the theory that the evolution of literature branches out into new experiments, and always follows the line of those experiments, seems to me to be flatly contradicted by all the facts of literary history. It seems to me an objective fact quite apart from my own preferences; indeed, it sometimes goes against my own preferences. Crashaw and the Cavalier mystics were, in the best sense of the word, fantastics. They were fantastics of whose fantasy I am very fond. But they did not lead away English literature indefinitely to be more and more fantastic; to indulge more and more in topsy-turvy tropes and far-fetched conceits. In a generation or so, English literature was back in the channel that was normal; indeed, rather too normal. It was that poetry of good sense which began in the maturity of Dryden and died on the birthday of Burns.

Nobody knows what will be the fashion a hundred years hence, except that it will almost certainly not be anything that is considered the newest fashion today. If I know that a river has wandered in winding curves from its original fountain, I may be quite unable to guess where it eventually wanders after it has passed where I stand. The one thing I can be fairly sure of is that it will not suddenly begin to go quite straight like a canal. As a mere matter of guess-work, given the tendencies of our time, I should think it would be extremely probable that literature will give up all this notion of experiment, and not only return to type, but even to the classical type. I think it much more likely that there will then be a worship of Landor, for instance, or some rather neglected classical classic, than that the whole world will be looking back to Miss Stein as the mother of modern English prose. We see the tendency in the Thomists of France, in the Humanists of America, and I think it is likely to become rather more classical than I like. For I am a romantic person myself; and I also like my little joke, just like Miss Stein.

I WAS recently enjoying a book published some little time ago, under the name of *The Stuffed Owl; an Anthology of Bad Verse.* The specimens were selected, I think, by Mr. D. B. Wyndham Lewis and Mr. Lee; but I am not reviewing the work, which must have been reviewed everywhere long ago, and has, I trust, received the admiration it certainly deserves. For the moment it has merely sent my wits wandering in the wide and rich and many-coloured fields of inferior literature. Much have the editors of the anthology travelled in these realms of gold; and I do not dream of competing with their deep scholarship touching the monumental classics of bad writing, or their exquisite and delicate artistic instinct for the finest and freshest shades of imbecility. If I may reverently adapt Matthew Arnold's definition of culture, they do indeed know the worst that has been said and thought in the history of humanity. Of course, any critic can complain of any anthology that some of his own favourites have been left out. He may sometimes even claim that some that are not on the high level of the anthology have been put in. As the critic skims an ordinary anthology to find an item which he can condemn as a blemish, so here the critic may pounce upon something that is not sufficiently half-witted to satisfy his high standard, and sternly point to several passages that are not so bad as they should be. Glimmerings of almost human intelligence, gleams of more than merely bestial reason, spasms of something almost resembling speech, relieve the monotony of the Imperial poems of Alfred Austin or the pagan passions of the more fearless, not to say shameless, imitators of Swinburne. Every now and then, after wading through a hubbub of hundreds of words, we find a word that seems to have gone right by accident. We must not complain; nothing in this mortal life is perfect; not even bad poetry.

Of course, there is one real difficulty in the classification of such classics. They necessarily divide themselves into at least two distinct types, which have really a rather different status and value. They raise two questions, which are hardly of equal intellectual importance. The first is: "Why do people who are not poets try to write poetry?" The second is: "Why do people who are poets fail to write poetry?" It is the second question which is the more difficult to answer and therefore the more worth answering. The first class consists of any number of accidents of ignorance and inexperience and vanity

and egotistical self-deception; but beyond that there is
nothing very extraordinary about it. A mysterious
proverb declares that little birds who can sing and won't
sing must be made to sing; though I never could
imagine how. But evidently nobody ever had the courage
to suggest what should be done with little birds who
can't sing and do sing. There seems no suggestion possible, except that they should be shot; against which,
in the name of St. Francis, the patron of all birds, poets,
and other minor nuisances, I warmly protest. Of this sort
of merely provincial limitation, the poetry of the Village
Bard who looks dreadfully like the Village Idiot, the
sort of thing that Oliver Wendell Holmes playfully
satirized in the character of Gifted Hopkins, there is,
of course, a great deal in such an anthology as this. There
is a lot of it in the book; but there is also such a lot of
it in the world that the examples must almost necessarily
be accidents. Each one of us has probably found his own
favourite piece of folly, in an advertisement or an epitaph
or a corner of a newspaper; and the thing has remained
almost as private as a family joke. To keep a record of
all these individual discoveries would need not an
anthology but a library of lunacy; a Bodleian of Bad
Verse.

I cannot resist the temptation of telling Mr. D. B.
Wyndham Lewis, and all other true lovers of bad poetry,

of one poet to whom I know they would not refuse the laurel. He was so famous a person as the Rev. Patrick Brontë, the father of the great Brontë sisters; and his verses are actually printed along with theirs at the end of one edition of their works. He has often been called harsh and inhuman; but he deserves a place in literature since he invented a metre that is an instrument of torture. It consists of a rhyming verse finally ending on a word which ought to rhyme and does not. He is describing, if I remember right, the ideal virtues of the Village Maiden, and one verse runs—

> To novels and plays not inclined
> Nor aught that can sully her mind;
> Temptations may shower,
> Unmoved as a tower
> She quenches the fiery arrows.

It is long since I have sat at the feet of this minstrel; and I quote from memory; but I think another verse of the same poem thus illustrated the same paraprosdokian, or concluding jerk of disappointment—

> Religion makes beauty enchanting;
> And even where beauty is wanting,
> The temper and mind
> Religion-refined
> Will shine through the veil with sweet lustre.

If you read much of it, you will reach a state of mind in which, even though you know the jolt is coming, you can hardly forbear to scream. We have read much of the gloomy life of the Brontë sisters in their dark and narrow house, on their sombre and savage moorlands. We have heard a great deal of how their souls were attuned to the storm, whether of wild winds or of stern words. But I can imagine no storm so paralysing as the noise of a reverend gentleman reading that poem; no torture so savage as the ruthless repetition of that metre; no inhuman cry so awful or so freezing to the blood, even out of the very heart of the hell of *Wuthering Heights*. In spite of all the educationists, it is a kindness to children to teach them nursery rhymes. But a man ought to be imprisoned for Cruelty to Children, if he recited to them rhymes that do not rhyme.

But the problem is much more interesting if we leave the bad poetry written by bad poets, and come to the bad poetry written by good poets. It is an old story; it was Horace, I think, who said that Homer sometimes nods; and Horace, though a wideawake sort of person, sometimes indulged in a wink. The Swan of Avon, the Nightingale of Burford, the Skylark for whom we can name no habitation but the sky, all these famous birds occasionally threatened to stiffen into the Stuffed Owl. Even Milton, who lived for the grand style, had lapses of good taste; at least, I, for one, never liked Satan inventing gunpowder or spreading an extra special champagne supper, in the style of the Ritz-Carlton, to stay the hunger of the human Christ for bread. It is, therefore, no disrespect to great poets to make them figure in this book of bad poetry; for there is hardly a single good poet who has not at some time been a bad poet. I am not sure of the meaning of this, but I am fairly sure, for practical purposes, of the moral of it. First of all, it is wholesome to note that the poet generally came a cropper when he was moving most smoothly on the butter-slide of praise and progress and the prevailing fashion. It is when the classical poet is most classical that he strikes us as pompous and vapid. It is when the romantic poet is most romantic that he strikes us as sloppy and sentimental. And it will be when the modern poet is most modern, when he is most arrestingly in the modern style, that he will strike posterity as merely dowdy and dull. The only two really bad lines in Swinburne are the most Swinburnian; that couplet about lilies and langours and raptures and roses. By being in a sense perfect Swinburne, it shows up Swinburne as imperfect. And the other moral is that poets are men; and that men can no longer be worshipped as gods. Carlyle did his worst work when he resurrected the pagan term of Hero-Worship. The Pagans, indeed, put up a statue to Achilles; but they did not whitewash the statue. They had an objective way with them, which needed no moral self-deception. But Carlyle could not be a Pagan; he could only be a bad Christian; or, as some say, a Puritan. And he did whitewash Cromwell and Frederick, as nobody whitewashed Achilles. Shakspere and Shelley were better than Cromwell and Frederick; but they also were men and not statues. Even their bad poetry may be productive of good philosophy.

It was said of Miss Arabella Allen, that pioneer of Feminism, that she didn't know what she did like, but did know what she didn't like. Many very recent pioneers resemble her, which is odd. A little while ago, all liberal and cultured persons were expected to agree that negative morality was nothing as compared with positive morality. Enlightened clergymen took a pride in removing the Ten Commandments from their altars and their sermons, and substituting those two great mystical commands concerning the positive duties of the love of God and Man. Famous and fashionable writers, like Stevenson, spoke for their generation in saying: "Christ would not hear of negative morality; 'Thou shalt' was ever his word." Some enthusiasts carried the distinction to rather fantastic lengths, elaborately framing sentences from which negatives were excluded. When Tommy twisted the cat's tail, they twisted the English tongue to invent a dissuasion that should not be in the form of a negative. Instead of saying, "Do not twist the cat's tail," they said, "Do, do show a positive benevolence to animals," or words to that effect. Rushing into the nursery, just in time to prevent the new toy chisel from the little tool-card being driven into the little sister's eye, they yet had time hastily to rearrange their words and sentences, to avoid saying, "Don't do that," and say instead, "Occupy yourself in some other fashion," or "Employ your tools in the delightful craft of carpentry."

But, though the theory had its extremists, like other theories, it was no doubt a healthy reaction at the time it occurred. It was a reaction from Puritanism, and especially from dead Puritanism, which had dried up into a few negative commands and nothing else. Even when it was at its best, I confess I had some doubts about it. Indeed, I sometimes feared that it might mask the return of a positive Puritanism more terrible than negative Puritanism. At least if the authority only said, "Do not burn down the house," we may lawfully infer that we are allowed to do anything else with it; as, for instance, to paint it sky-blue with yellow stripes; or turn it into a public house or a castle defended by cannon. If no other veto is laid upon us except "Do not wake the baby," it follows that any silent and stealthy occupation, such as directing a smooth and soundless flow of treacle into the works of the piano, or cutting off all the hair of all the little girls next door and turning it into artificial beards for private theatricals—it follows, I say, that all these mute but active forms of energy were tacitly permitted.

I am not sure that the very fact that negative morality has a narrower scope does not sometimes mean that it leaves a wider liberty. If there are only Ten Commandments, it means that there are only ten things forbidden; and that means that there are ten million things that are not forbidden. Let us do justice to our ancestors, if they found it easier and shorter to describe what they forbade than what they permitted. Nevertheless, with all these correctives and criticisms, the idea was fundamentally sound; it was, as I have said, the very right instinct that a religion is dead when it has ceased to dwell on the positive and happy side of its visions, and thinks only of the stern or punitive side. Anyhow, right or wrong, it was prevalent through the whole of what may be called the progressive period. It was almost the mark of an emancipated and hopeful person that he insisted that we must think first of positive good, rather than of negative evil.

And that is what makes the present position so very queer. In the very latest phase of literature, especially in the literature of satire or social criticism, we find exactly the contrary. We find the most modern writers have lost exactly what progress promised to give them, and have kept exactly what progress threatened to destroy. What I mean, for instance, is something roughly like this. Charles Dickens was not a philosopher; he most certainly was not a theologian, not even a moral theologian; only, it may be said, in a casual and popular sense a moralist. But suppose we took in detail all the destructive fun and farce of Dickens, all his devastating portraits of oily philanthropists and bumptious social bullies; all the prigs and privileged bigwigs and blustering obstructive officials whom he pilloried in a hundred places. Suppose in any such time and place we had stopped him and said, "But what do you want? What is your ideal? What would you substitute for all this? Under whom would you put Oliver Twist, if not under Bumble? Where would you send Smike except to Squeers? What ought Mrs. Jellyby to consider, if not Africa? To whom ought Mrs. Weller to listen, if not to Mr. Stiggins? What politics are right, if Dedlock's are wrong? What morals are right, if Gradgrind's are wrong?" I think it practically certain that Dickens would answer, and even answer promptly. Some of his remarks would strike some of his hearers as having the limits or illusions of his time; as, for instance, he might believe more in the Radical reforms and education which were then beginning than some of us do who have seen them in their ending. Other remarks might shock other hearers, by their still more shocking and disgusting devotion to barbarous idolatries and superstitions; as, for instance, to the idea of the Family or even the institution of Marriage. For I fear it is only too probable that Dickens would advance the grotesque plea that Mrs. Jellyby ought to think about Mr. Jellyby, and that even Mrs. Weller might occasionally listen to Mr. Weller. But whether his replies were revoltingly reactionary in this way, or merely a little too contented with the jog-trot reforms of his own day, I say that Dickens would reply, and would find no difficulty in replying.

Now, if we take a satirist of the modern moment, even a man of genius or genuine intellectual activity, like Mr. Aldous Huxley or Mr. Percy Wyndham Lewis, I am not so certain that they could reply. Some of them see with extraordinary vividness the humbug or impudence or intellectual cruelty of this or that social type, in this or that social situation. But suppose we answered them by saying, "This moralist is a humbug, but what morality should a man preach, in order not to be a humbug? This positive claim is impudent, but can you be positive without being impudent? Many situations are cruel to many people; state briefly how you would be kind to these people." I have a very strong suspicion that our modern moral satirists would be entirely stumped. Things are very complex, and everybody is doing the wrong thing; but I suspect they really think that things are too complex for anybody to do the right thing. Therefore there is a hollow in the heart of their whirlwind of destructive criticism, as there is a hollow in the heart of the whirlpool. I do not mean it metaphorically, as suggesting that they are hollow in the sense of false. I mean it almost actually; that they are hollow and know they are hollow, and even admit they are hollow, as a hungry man would admit he was hollow. They have not enough solid sustenance; not enough food for the mind, as distinct from acrobatic exercise for the mind. I do not, as some do, denounce all these modern moralists as immoral. I only say that the most modern moralists are now at one with the most antiquated moralists. Like their Puritan great-grandfathers, they have nothing but negative morality.

THE greatness of the great Jonathan Swift grows upon me as I go on through life, like a man travelling nearer and nearer to a mountain. I did not understand him when I was very young; which is not to be wondered at, seeing that most people understood him so little as to give me his *Gulliver's Travels* as a book written for children. Also he was hidden from me by the rather hypocritical haze of literary sentiment which pervaded the Victorian time. It was, in this case, very largely a stale political prejudice, due to the fact that Swift had been a Tory and that the whole Victorian legend was a sort of triumph of the Whigs. I began to learn better the more I learned about his period, and to learn better still, the more I learned about my own. For Swift stood at the beginning of something of which (it may be) we stand at the end; the whole of that cycle of commercial Imperialism and commercial Parliamentarism which he already distrusted at its very beginning, or before it had really begun. Anyhow, I learned to like Swift for all the things for which Macaulay and Thackeray disliked him. I liked him for liking Bolingbroke; for despising

Marlborough; for showing up the Glorious Hanoverian Succession in Ireland as a very low and dirty job; for treating the wit of the Freethinkers with contempt; for giving the first place to the virtue of Honour, which practically disappeared from politics and financial affairs about this time. It is doubtless true that he was too bitter and exclusive, but that is no reason why we should be. And the final phase of true philanthropy is not complete until it can love the misanthrope.

But I have often noticed a rather curious fact or fancy. Whenever there is a sort of proverb or anecdote or allusion, always connected with a literary man in literary gossip, that proverb always misses the point. So many people could hardly mention Dr. Johnson without the highly irrelevant remark that he wrote a Dictionary. So the favourite or fashionable phrase about Dean Swift seemed to be that he "wrote an essay on a Broomstick." Indeed, the literary gossip managed to miss the point even here. The real point of the essay on a Broomstick is not merely that it is on a Broomstick, but that it is an essay in parody or satire upon the essays of Boyle, the most fashionable writer of the day. As for broomsticks, I imagine that Swift could have written a hundred essays on a hundred broomsticks. Nor do I see any particular reason why it should be difficult; many people could do it; I could do it myself. For, to begin with, almost any

subject, considered as a subject, contains stuff and sub-
stance enough for an essay, when we consider that its
origin and object, and material and design, and relation
to other things, are all subjects in themselves. And
secondly, a broomstick does not strike me as being
intrinsically a dull subject, but rather a romantic one.
The picturesque aspects of it, that leap into sight at
once, so to speak, would suffice for an essay much longer
than Swift's. A broom, and consequently, a broomstick,
are connected with religious ideas of purification, and
with other ideas which are rather the reverse. George
Herbert dedicated the broom especially to the service of
God. The witches dedicated the broomstick especially
to the service of Satan. And if the essayist is so fastidious as to find the subject of devil-worship merely mild
and tame, we might well ask what subjects he finds
sensational or exciting. There are a hundred other things
to be said, of course, even without plagiarizing from
Swift. The image applied to politics, in some places,
might even be alarmingly significant. The broomstick
is a bundle of twigs decidedly suggestive of the *Fasces*,
and quite a number of things might be written about
that.

But this rather misleading though traditional trifle
has another interest for the imagination. Swift, as I
have said, was a man who could write what nobody

else could have written, and often at a time when nobody else would have dared to write it. He could write the truth about a time in which perhaps more lies were told, and about which perhaps more lies have since been taught, than any other episode in English history. He could say the right thing, and say it exactly rightly; with a deadly detachment or a stunning understatement unmatched in the satires of mankind. But Swift was not a man gifted with the particular grace with which this literary legend would distinguish him. He was not a man who specially saw a spiritual significance in common things, or learned great lessons from small objects, or had anything about him of the poet who finds poetry in prose. He was a religious man in an irreligious age; but only because he was really too intellectual a man to be merely an irreligious man. He had nothing about him of the mystic, who sees divine symbols everywhere, who turns a stone and starts a wing. There were only too many stones, and not half enough wings, in poor Jonathan Swift's existence, and I fear he was largely saved from scepticism by a contempt for the sceptics. He did not see the glory of God in a broomstick; but he did see something very like a broomstick in the stuck-up wooden-headed young atheist who denied the glory of God. He did see that the ideas in the head of that philosophical broomstick were all tied together as loosely as a bundle of sticks, and that these borrowed notions bore the same relation to real sincerity and originality as the twigs tied on to a broomstick bear to the branches growing on a tree. In short, his approach to such central truths was noble indeed, but somewhat narrow and negative; he was wise by the follies of others; or at any rate, not merely out of the wisdom that is at one with charity. And because he was partly deficient in charity he was really deficient in poetry, though certainly not deficient in fancy. He was the last person in the world to write a poem about a broomstick; yet a hundred minor poets, so long as they were poets, could easily imagine a poem about a broomstick. Why, even the Nursery Rhymes have already set us a most spirited example, in that imaginative flight that swept the starry spiders' webs out of the very corners of the sky.

It is perhaps worth while to note this incongruity about the literary legend, because it will soon be necessary to insist that each of these talents exists and each is valuable to truth. In the somewhat acid mood that is coming upon men of letters just now, it is likely enough that they will return to the realism of the great satirist, and accept his limitations along with his liberties. They will begin to be just to Swift, and immediately begin to be unjust to Blake or Wordsworth or Walt Whitman. For they seem unable to believe that different literary virtues are needed to balance each other; and a great deal of contemporary criticism reads to me like a man saying: "Of course I do not like green cheese; I am very fond of brown sherry."

I HAVE already remarked on the American cult called Humanism. It is the creation of certain critics who, broadly speaking, would substitute a certain classicism, such as is found in the ancients, for both the romanticism and realism of the moderns. There are those, of course, who call classicism cold, especially those who like their own realism or romanticism hot and strong. As a matter of fact, classicism is by no means the vital thing in Humanism. It is especially not the human thing in Humanism. I am by no means sure that I should myself agree with the Humanist leaders in everything. But I do most heartily agree with them in one thing, and it seems to me very much the most important thing. It is substantially this. The Humanist says to the Humanitarian, "You are always telling me to forget divine things and think of human things. And then you talk to me eagerly and earnestly about the pathetic helplessness of human beings, their faulty environment, their fatal heredity, their obvious animal origins, their uncontrollable animal instincts, ending with the old fatalist cry that we must forgive everything because there is nothing to forgive. But these things are not the *human* things. These are specially and specifically the sub-human things; the things we share with nature and the animals. The specially and outstandingly human things are exactly the things that you dismiss as merely divine things. The human things are free will and responsibility and authority and self-denial, because they exist only in humanity."

Upon this pivotal point I am entirely at one with Humanism, but I do not propose to discuss that particular point here. I only wish to record an impression about some of the more violent opponents of Humanism, and especially upon one phrase which abounds in their phraseology and presumably means something in their philosophy. Many who can look back on long and happy lives passed in the character of Young Rebels are very much annoyed at the appearance of this antiquated classicism, especially when it appears (as it generally does) in people rather younger than themselves. And I notice that the slogan to be used against the Humanist is to consist in saying that they are merely Critical, whereas all the people who happen to dislike them are Creative. And, though I have no intention of getting into a quarrel about the word Humanism, I do feel somewhat attracted to an attempt to consider what we mean, and especially what they mean, by the words

Creative and Critical.

I take it that the disparagement of the Critical, as compared with the Creative, does not mean that nobody must be allowed to write unless he writes novels; that it is a sufficient condemnation to say that Professor Paul Elmer More has not yet written a murder story, or Professor Babbitt knocked the town endways with a roaring farce. The Humanists are human beings; that, at least, may be tentatively conceded to them; and human beings are allowed to think, even while they do not carve, paint, build, or play the fiddle. But when we consider Creation with a significance a little deeper, we find it a little more difficult. It is much too difficult to dogmatize about; nor am I dogmatizing: I am only asking questions, like Socrates, of people whom I suspect of not knowing what their own dogmas are. What exactly do these exquisitely modern moderns mean when they say that their modern literature is Creative? I strongly suspect that, even when it is clever, it is emphatically not Creative. It is exactly what it accuses its enemies of being: it is Critical. For instance, I have a hearty admiration for the amazing vitality and veracity of much of the work of Mr. Aldous Huxley. I think he is the most brilliant of the moderns; and he is admittedly one of the most modern of the moderns. But his work, considered as an intellectual process, seems to me almost entirely Critical.

Of course, it is not easy to point to anything that is entirely Creative. In ultimate philosophy, as in ultimate theology, men are not capable of creation, but only of combination. But there is a workable meaning of the word, which I take to be this: some image evoked by the individual imagination which might never have been evoked by any other imagination, and adds something to the imagery of the world. I call it Creative to write "the multitudinous seas incarnadine." I call it Creative by three real and even practical tests: first, that nobody need ever have thought of such a thing if Mr. William Shakspere had not happened to think of it; second, that while it is an apocalyptic, or titanic, it is not really an anarchic idea; it is gigantic, but it does not merely sprawl; it fits into the frame of thought exactly as the sea fits into all the fretted bays and creeks of the world. Also, in passing, with all its tragic occasion, it is a *jolly* image: it gives the mere imagination a positive and passionate joy of colour, like the joy of drinking a purple sea of wine. But, thirdly and most essentially, it does reveal the moral mystery that is the whole meaning of such a tragedy; expressed by the knocking without which startles the assassins within; the notion of the thin partition between the crime that is hidden in the house and the sin that fills the universe; what was meant by saying that things said in the inner chamber should be proclaimed from the housetops; the true idea of the Day of Judgment, in which the world is, really and truly, turned inside out. It may also be added that that astonishing phrase is not only a speech, but a gesture. It is dramatic, in the vital sense, to suppose that dipping a finger could suddenly turn all the seas of the world to scarlet. But this very drama is a morality, and it would mean nothing that the seas were scarlet unless the sins were scarlet. . . . But what is all this? This is not Modern. This is not Scientific. This is not in the purely experimental and realistic manner in which the Young Rebels have been writing for the last thirty or forty years. They all say they are Creative, and they ought to know. And, according to their theory of purely Creative art, there ought to be an entirely detached and unmoral attitude on the part of everybody involved. It ought not to matter whether the spot on Lady Macbeth's finger was blood or red ink; or whether she turned the multitudinous seas the colour of carnage or tomato soup. It is evidently a very soothing and insulated condition of intellect, and avoids all the disturbing currents of ethical and theological criticism. There is nothing to be said against it; except that, if everybody were in that scientific state of mind, nobody could write *Macbeth*.

And there, as it seems to me, the whole theory of uncritical and uncriticized creative art breaks down. As a mere matter of fact, you cannot make any sense of *Macbeth* unless you not only recognize but share a decided horror of murder. And how you can be shocked by Murder and not moved by Morality I do not know. And if being Critical means the tracing of these electric wires or burglar-alarms, these live wires of the laws of life which do, in fact, give shocks when they are touched or transgressed, then it is not merely the classical critics who are critical. It is Shakspere who is critical; nay, it is Lady Macbeth who is critical; she is extremely critical of Lady Macbeth. If the recognition of the real Ten Commandments of life and death is only being critical, then all the great creative artists are critical; and they would not be creative if they were not critical. Lady Macbeth would never see that blasting vision of a bloodshot world, except in the last agony of self-criticism.

In these times when everybody is talking about taxation, many must have indulged in the dream that there might be a tax on talking. I hasten (nay, rush in a rage of self-immolation) to add that the same may be said of a tax on writing. We have endeavoured to preserve the old liberal ideal of free speech and free printing, at least in its legal form, if sometimes as a legal fiction. I fear that the truth is not so much that repression is entirely removed, as that repression is not responsible repression. Like so many other things, it has begun to act outside the limits of law, and tyranny as well as liberty has broken loose. Repression is irresponsible, and therefore repression itself is irrepressible. Private powers acting as public powers, monopolies, boycotts, big shops, publishing syndicates, and similar things do, in fact, inflict restriction which we should not allow the State or the Church to inflict. But even the most earnest eleutheromaniac may allow himself a day-dream of abstract possibilities. And, if we agree that the State must not attack expression with the old weapon of punishment, we might toy with the fancy of attacking it with the new method of monetary rating. Nobody now wishes men to be tortured for talking nonsense, but they might be taxed for talking nonsense. Indeed, in these days, when so many schools give Lessons in Citizenship, most people seem to be so vague about such things that they would hardly know the difference. A citizen can hardly distinguish between a tax and a fine, except that the fine is generally much lighter.

Of course, there is a sort of paradox in taxation, anyhow. In such a tax, there is often the notion of checking something, and yet the hope that it will not be checked. A lover of birds might wish to have a tax on cats, with the idea that there would be fewer cats. But the statesman imposing the tax would presumably hope that the streets would be thronged with thousands and thousands of cats, each bringing its little subscription to the embarrassed Exchequer. Now, it seems illogical to wish to moderate the influx of cats and not to wish to moderate the influence of tigers. Yet it is very unlikely that the State will ever put a tax on tigers; because, alas! these beautiful creatures are rare in our English lanes and still rarer by our English firesides. Any lover of nature who has seen the first tiger appearing somewhat prematurely in early spring will almost certainly (if he survives) write a letter to the newspapers about it, as an event even more exceptional than the cuckoo. There is not enough money in tigers to make it worth while to tax them; so that in cases of that sort we cannot act upon the principle of the check or public protection alone.

But, for the sake of argument, we will leave out in this light speculation all the purely economic considerations arising from the width of the taxable area. It would obviously be impossible, as well as iniquitous, to tax the sort of remarks that are made as a part of the ordinary round of social life. To impose even a light tax on every repetition of the expression "It's a fine day," or "It's a strange world," or "Nothing doing in the City," or "Pint of bitter, Miss," or any of those great pivotal utterances on which all human life revolves, would be outside the sphere of practical politics. The sort of talk to be taxed must be something sufficiently widespread to be worth taxing, but something sufficiently superfluous to suffer even a prohibitive tax without the world being much the worse.

In fact, the tax on talk may well follow the rough distinction already recognized about necessities and luxuries. The pint of bitter, the word about the weather, are necessities. For the poor, beer is a necessity, as tobacco is very nearly a necessity; it is only for people sufficiently rich and fashionable to be faddists that either is really a luxury. In the same way, a certain sort of primeval and eternal gossip is a necessity. But there are all sorts of things that are not necessities. The mention of mere names seen in the newspapers; the oppressive presence of science, combined with the absence of knowledge; the habit we all have of talking about what we do not understand; all these might be smartly interrupted by the tax-collector coming round as the tram conductor comes round for fares.

For instance, suppose everybody was instantly fined a small sum for mentioning the name of Einstein. The money would be refunded if he could afterwards demonstrate, to a committee of mathematicians and astronomers, that he knew anything about Einstein. What a salutary check it would be on the public speaker, criticizing the Budget or the latest economic panacea, who would be just in the very act of saying: "Makes the brain reel. Reminds one of——" and would sharply catch himself up, with a holy fear of losing half a crown, and hastily substitute *Alice in Wonderland*. On the other hand, it would be equally valuable in arresting the headlong pen of the journalist announcing Brighter Brotherhood or reverently praising The Revolt of Youth: "The new year opens before us new faiths, new ideals, and the young will no longer be content with the dead shibboleths of creed and dogma. New light has been thrown on all the daily problems of life by the great scientific genius of our time; the name of——": and then he will stop suddenly and be most horribly stumped, for Einstein is the only man of science he has heard of, and Einstein costs two-and-six.

It is a luxury, in the strict sense of a superfluity, to mention Einstein. He is not a part of any ordinary human argument, because any ordinary human being does not know where his argument leads or what it can really be used to prove. It may be, for all I know, a perfectly good argument for those who really follow it; but those who drag in the name without the argument cannot know what an argument means. We should not be interfering with the freedom of debate by eliminating it, for the men who only deal in such unknown quantities are not debating. They are simply showing off. The distinguished name is stuck into the sentence as the diamond tie-pin is stuck into the tie, for the sake of swagger or snobbishness. And diamond tie-pins are quite legitimate objects for a tax on luxuries. Of course, the argument does not only apply to science; there are any number of cases of the same sort of pedantry in literature. There are certain quotations from poetry which are always dragged in as if they were texts of Scripture, professedly to prove something that obviously proves itself, but really to prove that the writer is well acquainted with the Hundred Best Authors.

The tax would have a refreshing and reviving effect

upon literature, because it would drive writers to think of a few new examples. The man who writes to show that Science was always persecuted in the past will be driven to the dreadful necessity of writing about somebody else besides Galileo. And who knows what a new life of brighter and brisker research into the elements of history the change may not mean for him! The man who is writing to show that poets always die young, or are killed by the critics, if he is absolutely forbidden (at the rate of five shillings) to say that the *Quarterly* was tartarly and ask, "What are Keats?" might discover all sorts of neglected poets; or, better still, discover that there were some poets who were not neglected. Those who can never separate Spain from the Spanish Inquisition, or America from the similar institution of Prohibition, or Russia from the German Jew called Karl Marx, might, at the price of a temporary tax on these topics, find out a good many other truths about these nations. They might find, for example, what Spain did in America; what America is doing in Russia; and whether all Russian peasants have really turned into German Jews.

ON re-reading something I wrote about the most modern poetry, especially touching the ancient riddle of Sense and Sound, I am not sure that I made myself clear. And, as I am not now writing the most modern poetry, I may be allowed to be clear. Clarity will be permissible, or at least pardonable. By the way (if I may mention it in parenthesis) does anybody know why it is now the fashion to be very extravagant in poetry and very sober in prose? There are individuals, of course, like Mr. James Joyce or Miss Gertrude Stein, whose prose may be said to be of doubtful sobriety. But some of the ablest of the rising, or recently risen, authors seem to have something like a dual personality in prose and verse. The prose-writing of Mr. Osbert Sitwell is not especially Sitwellian, as the term is applied to his poetry. It is well written, but rather on the old principle that a book well written should be as unobtrusive as a man well dressed. It is in the Sitwellian poesy that the average reader is apt to be startled by strange sights; by woolly roses or hairy clouds. Mr. T. S. Eliot's wildest verses do, indeed, have rhythm, too much rhythm;

really (as the phrase goes) making the head go round, and suggesting a cosy life in the hollow heart of a cyclone or a whirlpool. But there is nothing of this in his essays; which are rather contained and reticent than otherwise. Indeed, when he does make an epigram (and a very good one) he is so ashamed of it that he hides it at the end of a minute footnote, for fear some critic or other should accuse him of brilliancy.

The same is largely true even of Mr. Aldous Huxley, so far as essay-writing is concerned. His diaries of real travel are quite sensible and unpretentious; while some of his poems are like imaginary travels in the Tropics, almost negro in their barbaric dance of death. The Victorians, who are accused of primness, had much more all-round extravagance. George Meredith was as perverse and fanciful in prose as in verse; indeed, more so. Diana of the Crossways seemed to sit not so much at the cross-roads as in the heart of the labyrinth; and the Egoist juggled much more deceptively than Juggling Jerry. Some of Browning's friends complained that he was cryptic, not only in prose but in private correspondence. I am not complaining of this new method of making extremes meet. There may be a great deal to be said for it; but perhaps it means some decay of the Victorian *naturalness,* which was much more typical than the Victorian decorum. There is something to be said for Browning and Meredith, if only that they could not help writing like Meredith and Browning.

But this (as I say) is all in brackets. The matter I meant to raise concerns sense and sound in poetry. And their relation is much more subtle than even the most insanely subtle of the critics seem to understand. I took the familiar example of a famous line in Milton, which has always had that inexplicable fascination so often found in the purely classical style. Oddly enough, it is in the rational lines of Virgil or Milton, much more than in the extra-rational lines either of the Merediths or the Sitwells, that we feel the final mystery of song; the something that instantly gives delight and escapes from definition; the thing of which we say: "I cannot tell, for the life of me, why that is so good as it is." I cannot tell, for the life of me, why the line "Like Teneriffe or Atlas unremoved" is as good as it is. Yet it is perfectly straightforward; it merely mentions a cape and a mountain, and adds the somewhat superfluous information that they are not removed. The only thing I am quite sure about is that the sense depends on the sound and the sound depends on the sense. It actually would not sound the same, if another meaning were expressed by the same sound. It actually would not mean as much, if other words expressed the same meaning. It would be easy enough to try the experiment in a rough and ready way. It is obvious that, if we wrote "Like Beachy Head or Snowdon unremoved," it would not be within a thousand miles of the thing; though Beachy Head is a cape and Snowdon is a mountain. What is not quite so obvious is that the converse is also true. It might be too lightly inferred that the mere noise of the names is alone majestic. It might be even suggested that the down-rushing dactyl of "Teneriffe" has some faint echo of words like "terrible" or "towering," and that the sound is the secret. But it is not so, though the alternative experiment might be a little more elaborate to construct. Let us have a stab at it, as Mr. P. G. Wodehouse's young man said when asked if he would be a reasonable being.

Thackeray mentions somewhere, in one of his essays, that in some old cookery-book or book of etiquette he had come on the fact that men in the eighteenth century drank a wine called Teneriffe, apparently an alternative to port or Madeira. Thackeray says, I think, that it sounds like having to swallow the Matterhorn. But if it were something quite familiar, like port wine, it would sound like any other detail of the dinner-table. As for the word "Atlas," we have only to knock out the capital letter, and it means a commonplace work of reference, an ordinary book of maps. Now, suppose somebody were writing a very mild and jog-trot domestic poem in deca-

syllabics, rather like those poems in which Cowper celebrated the tea-urn or the cat. And suppose the particular
passage explained how somebody's after-dinner table was
left in a litter by negligent servants; books and wine and
everything in a hugger-mugger—

> His pipe and napkin, like his spectacles,
> Like snuff and toast and pen and ink or books,
> Like teneriffe or atlas, unremoved.

It would not make the same noise. It actually would not
sound in the ear, as a matter of mere acoustics, the same.
The fact of talking only about two trivial objects would,
in fact, alter the actual impact of the sound upon the ear
and the nerves. Nobody would be looking for a great
sonorous effect, and nobody would find it. The fact that
the two objects are mountains, mysterious and remote
and legendary mountains, does enter irrevocably into the
merely physical process; and it is the largeness of those
mountains that fills the lungs and the ear.

This being so, I think there are much deeper difficulties than are now generally understood about breaking with the traditions of rhythm. I do not say it should
not be done, but I do say that it is doubtful whether
those who do it know what they are doing. If my own
original use of this quotation was obscure, I am well
aware that the whole problem is one of the deepest ob-

scurity. But this is more or less what I meant; that I do not think we have got to anything like the bottom of the psychology—we might even say the physiology—of poetical effects; and that the old conventions of verse rested upon instincts which are perhaps indestructible, but which at least cannot be casually destroyed. It would seem that one growth can grow into another, even if they did originally have separate roots, in such a fashion as to form a single life and a new creation; and that new creation is none the less unique because it is now old. It is really beside the mark to talk about experiments which are only explosions; for, though explosions ought to be expansions, it is certain at least that they are disruptions. I do not object to experiments as such. I willingly agree that Mr. Sitwell has as much right to talk about a hairy cloud as an old poet to talk about a fleecy cloud; as much right to do what he can with the hair of a cloud as the other with the hair of a comet. But something much deeper and more mysterious is involved. The old poets had a power of mixing with their fleecy clouds and hairy comets some ancestral magic of the nature of music; by which even the quaintest of Cavalier conceits, or the most newly coined of Renaissance Latinisms, came weighted with harmonies and a historic richness that prevented them from being crude, even when they were new. It seems to me that the new poets do not try to recover that ancient wedding of sound and sense. Some of them seem to have only passed from the old Swinburnian phase of sound without sense to the later phase of nonsense without sound. But even the best of them seem to be seeking a divorce rather than a wedding.

MANY are complaining of the cliques in the literary world; and they are right for a particular reason, though I am not sure that they know it. The discontent, like so many of the present discontents, has a certain disadvantage; that it does not distinguish between the normal nuisances of human life and the special nuisances of modern life. Under no conditions should we all be equally in touch with each other, or distributing dispassionate justice to every human being like a Day of Judgment. It is natural for men to belong to a club, as it is natural for other men who do not belong to a club to call it a clique; and a great deal of what is called log-rolling is as easy as falling off a log. I have generally found that it was precisely because a man was generously and enthusiastically rolling the log of a friend that he complained so bitterly of the log-rolling among his enemies. But I am not forbidden to find that a writer is intelligent, even if he is my friend. I am permitted, perhaps, the vanity of supposing that he is my friend because he is intelligent; or at least that he became my friend partly because I thought he was intelligent. The relation is obviously open to abuse; and the method which I myself have always chosen is to praise the merit of a friend's public work as warmly as I felt inclined, but always to mention the private friendship as well as the public merit. Then anybody is free to discount it, if he thinks it ought to be discounted. But there is another and more neglected evil in the clique; in the club that cultivates some special variety in culture. The artists of such a group have a tendency not only to talk shop, but to talk workshop. They talk more about methods of production than about products of perfection. Like talkative art-students, they show each other their work before it is finished; and, like lazy art-students, they often find this an excellent excuse for not finishing it at all.

Perfect work is for the world; yes, for the stupid world. Imperfect work is for the class, for the club, for the clique; in a word, for the sympathizers. We show our worst efforts to the intelligent; we reserve our best efforts for the dull—that is, for the supreme and sacred duty of all creative expression; that of being sufficiently pointed to pierce at last even the mind of the dull. For, whatever be the nature of creation, it is certainly of the nature of translation; it is translating something from the dumb alphabet and dim infantile secret language in our own souls into the totally different public language that we talk with our tongues. If that translation were perfect, if the ideas and idioms did really correspond correctly, it would all be as plain to the man in the street as to the man in the club. It certainly would not be necessary to show it in fragmentary hints to the man in the clique. But because our expression is imperfect we need friendship to fill up the imperfections. A man of our own type or tastes will understand our meaning before it is expressed; certainly a long time before it is perfectly expressed. Thus we rather tend to lose the old idea that it is the business of the author to explain himself. We tend to adopt the idea that it is the business of the clique to understand the author; and even to explain the author, when he refuses to explain himself.

A famous æsthete of the 'nineties said that the poet who was admired by poets must be the greatest of poets. I will take the liberty to doubt it. I fancy that in such a case the poets are in fact collaborating with the poet. The beauty they behold in his work is partly their work as well as his. Just as the poets may see more than others see in every bush or cloud, so they may see more than others see in every epithet or metaphor. Above all, if they are poets of his own particular school of poetry, they will guess something of what he means by the queerest epithet or the maddest metaphor. But it does not follow that those words are the full and perfect expres-

sion of what he means; if they were, they probably
would not seem mad or even queer. In short, the poet
has not really travelled the whole of his pilgrimage from
Paradise to Putney (with apologies to the ghost of
Swinburne); an embassy of select and fastidious souls
of Putney has gone out and met him halfway. He has
not performed the full literary function of translating
living thoughts into literature. He still needs an inter-
preter; and a crowd of interpreters has officiously rushed
between the poet and the public. The crowd is the
clique; and it does do a certain amount of harm, I think,
by thus intercepting the true process of the perfecting
of human expression. It is not wrong because it en-
courages the great man to talk. It is wrong because it
actually discourages the great man from talking plainly.
The priests and priestesses of the temple take a pride in
the oracle remaining oracular. That vast but vague revolution that we call the modern world largely began about
the time when men demanded that the Scriptures should
be translated into English. It has ended in a time when
nobody dares to demand that English poets should be
translated into English. It has ended in a new race of
pedants who are only too proud of reading the poet in
the original, and merely murmur as they read, in a
tantalizing fashion, that the original is so very original.

This is the paradox of the clique; that it consists of

those who understand something and do not wish it to be understood; do not really wish it to be understandable. But such a group must in its nature be small, and its tendency is to make the range or realm of culture smaller. It consists of those who happen to be near enough to some unique or perverse mentality to guess that a man means something that as yet he cannot really say; just as a detective might be legitimately proud of having extracted some sort of valuable evidence from a lunatic who was deaf and dumb. But this does not make for the enlargement of the poet's power of expression or of the public's power of appreciation. The ideal condition is that the poet should put his meaning more and more into the language of the people, and that the people should enjoy more and more of the meaning of the poet. That is true popular education; and, if we really possessed that sort, we should hardly need any other. One party in the quarrel will insist that the public ought to take more trouble to understand the poet; and so it ought. But the other party can answer that the poet should take more trouble to finish his poems; and so he should. It is not a question of petty or conventional or finicking finish. It is a question of not leaving three-quarters of the poem inside the poet, with the rest of it hanging out, generally tail-foremost.

At present, even good poets often do not write good

poems, but rather notes for poems. They think it enough to record, as in a sort of disjointed diary, that they *did* feel a sense of poignant futility on seeing an old hat on a deserted hat-peg; or an indescribable surge of rebellion on observing a broken vase in a suburban dust-bin. And then comes the sympathetic critic, saying (no doubt quite truly) that he can imagine a man shuddering at the hat-peg or shedding tears into the dust-bin. But that is only saying that one individual can imagine the imagination. It is not completely communicating the imagination by means of the image. I am far from denying that a great poet might achieve a great turn of style, which would make something sublime out of a hat-peg or a dust-bin, as Shakspere did out of a bodkin or a bung-hole. But if such passages be examined, it will be found that nowhere did the great poet study the grand style more subtly than when dealing with such mean objects. Anyhow, he did not merely mention the mean objects, and then mention that they had filled him with feelings indescribable. He set out seriously to describe the indescribable. That is the whole business of literature, and it is a hard row to hoe.

I WAS recently asked to write a prologue to a composite
detective story, which demanded a detailed and vivid
description of the streets of Hong Kong. I have never
seen Hong Kong, and I have not the least notion of what
it looks like. But he would be a very faint-hearted journalist who should allow himself to be restrained from
realism and photographic exactitude by a trifle like that.
But, in the course of considering the matter, I fell into
a more general train of thought, to which Hong Kong
serves as a gate of entry, as it serves as a gate of entry
to China. Though I have never seen the mixed cosmopolitan ports of the Far East, I have seen some of the
yet more mixed and cosmopolitan ports of the Near
East. I have been in Port Said and Suez; and between
these and Hong Kong lies the whole vast and still
partly unknown thing that we call Asia. But my medi-
tations have overflowed upon this page, because they are
obviously too vague and general to be developed before
the innocent and happy spirits full of a beautiful eager-
ness to get on with the murder.

Whatever else the scribes have written about Asia,

they have all agreed in the statement that it is mysterious. It may seem perverse to say that this statement is
a mis-statement, or even that it is an over-statement.
Yet I think there is an aspect in which it can be contradicted. We may even say that the whole point of
Asia is that it is not mysterious; not half so mysterious
as Europe; to say nothing of America, which is the
most mysterious of all. By which I mean that there are
in Europe and America compromises and complexities,
a blend or balance of one thing with another, which is
really rather less apparent in the stark passions, the strict
rituals, and the ancient appetites of Asia. For instance,
a Christian is perpetually balanced between a Christian
ideal of loving his enemies, a Pagan ideal of punishing
his enemies, and a chivalric ideal of only fighting his
enemies fairly. In Asia, I imagine, both love and hate
have been much more unmixed and undisguised. Both
in poetry and in policy, a man would be much more
simple in his purpose to pursue his love or to persecute
his foe. And, while there is truth in the tradition that
the Asiatic has thus sometimes become an artist in sensu-
ality and an artist in cruelty, he might well make out
a case for the view that he was an artist with less artifice
and more sincerity. Somebody said, with considerable
truth, that Russia lacks the cement of hypocrisy. This
might well be quoted to support the not uncommon

view that Russia is a part of Asia.

It might be said that Asia is too old to be mysterious. It might at least be said that Asia is too old to be hypocritical. There are a thousand veils and disguises; but the disguises have worn very thin in thousands of years, and the veils are rather like the veils worn by loose women in Cairo and Port Said: ritual, but transparent. Those who would give a juvenile thrill by combining the occult and the obscene do still talk about the Mysteries of the Harem; the secrets behind the veils and curtains of the seraglio. But I imagine there is very little mystery about the harem, at any rate the Moslem harem; and no secret except the open secret. I imagine that the sentiments of the seraglio, whether domestic or servile or sensual, are often dull to that extreme point of dullness which the revolutionary West describes as respectable. I suspect that there is far more mystery, in the sense of mysticism, in the feelings of two common lovers in an English lane. It is only fair to add that, with all the ceremonial of reticence or invisibility, there is probably much less cant than there is in many an English novel or newspaper. But, whether it be subtlety or sophistry, whether it be hypocrisy or only human complexity, it is really in the West and not in the East that there is the mystery. The Occidental is always saying that he cannot understand the Oriental;

but the truth is that he cannot understand himself. It is the Christian culture that is woven of many strands, of many fabrics and colours, and twisted into the single knot, the knot that holds the world together, but the knot that is of all knots the most difficult to trace out or untie. Compared with that, there is something simple and smooth and all of a piece about the ancient silks of China or the peasant weaving of India. It is on the head of the Christian that the ends of the earth are come, even from the beginning, the arrows of the Persians or the stone clubs of the Celts. And if the eyelids are, after all, less weary than those of a Buddha or a Brahmin god, it may be that there is a slight fallacy in the familiar quotation, and that being hit on the head incessantly by the corners of the world does not merely send one to sleep. Anyhow, it is the Christian who is the real cosmic mystery; the cross made by the cross-lights of the shafts of the sunrise and the sunset; the true crux of the world. But it is only just to say that this complexity, which produces the highest philosophy, does also produce humbug. It produces the worst kind; in which the humbug hardly knows he is a humbug. I suspect that there is far less humbug in the East, and that, compared with such rooted and humanized humbug, all its cunning is a sort of simplicity.

In Asia things have worn too thin to be padded with such self-deception; it is old and its bones stick out. There the harlot is a harlot, and not a society actress whom the divorce court hands from one rich man to another. There the slave is a slave, and not a scheduled employee having less than the income nominated in the Act. There the king is a king, and the tyrant is a tyrant, and not a banker threatening to make nations bankrupt, or a private person holding all the shares in a public company. We have doubtless by our example introduced these blessings into Asia, but they are not Asiatic. There the usurer was a usurer, and the thief a thief; and this, which was the best thing about Asia, will probably be the one thing really altered by the influence of Europe. But it is worth while to say a word for the simplicity of Asia, and against the mystery of Asia. For on that supposed mystery of the East there has been erected every sort of quackery in the West. Every sham religion, every shabby perversion, every blackguard secret society, has claimed to feed on the strange fruits of that garden of Asia. And we may well hint that the garden itself is a little more decent, even if it is a desert.

There are any number of examples, both good and evil, of the sort of rigid simplicity that I mean, and

the sense in which the Orient has more simplicity than
secrecy. The Caste System of India, for instance, seems
to me to be a tyranny; and the worst sort of tyranny,
which is not conducted by a tyrant, but by an aristocracy: but it is not a hypocrisy. It is not even that more
confused and unconscious sort of hypocrisy that we call
humbug. It is not confused at all; its very cruelty is
in its clarity. You cannot play about with the idea of a
Brahmin as you can with the idea of a Gentleman. You
cannot pretend that Pariahs were made Pariahs entirely
as a compliment to them, and in the interests of True
Democracy. At least, if the Indians are talking like that
now, it is only too true that they have been infected
with the worst vices of the West. I wish I were sure
they were also being influenced by the real merits of the
West; and, above all, by this great merit of the West,
the name of which is Mystery. But it is they, the simple, who do not understand us, the mystical. A brilliant
and distinguished Hindu told me that the problem of
the world is to unite all things; that the things in which
they differ are indifferent, and only that things in which
they are the same are solid. I could not explain to him
that the problem of the Christian is not merely to unite
all things, but to unite union with disunion. The dif-
ferences are not indifferent; and the problem is to let
things differ while they agree. In short, the Western

man seeks after Liberty, which is a real mystery. Compared with that Unity is a platitude. It is the White Man who is the Dark Horse; and ourselves who are riddles to ourselves.

IT often happens that by-products are bigger than big production, and that side-issues are larger than the main issue. Much of the political muddle and squabble comes from people trying to reach what they call a practical agreement. It is a very unpractical thing to trust to practical agreement. Two people may agree to keep a cat; but if they only agree because one is a lover of animals, and the other has a fiendish pleasure in watching cruelty to birds, it is probable that the practical agreement will not last very long. Other occasions will arise, in which it will be found to suffer from the absence of a theoretical agreement. There is at this moment many a parley between two politicians, seeking to find a practical agreement about a Tax on Tobacco or the dumping of Danish bacon, who are, in fact, forbidden for ever to come to any kind of real agreement, for the simple reason that they live in two different worlds; as, for instance, one in the globe that is picked out in red patches of the British Empire, and the other in the great grey *orbis terrarum* in which all lands are alike. These men would really have to settle the big question before they settled the small question. But, in what we call practical politics, it is the small question that is called the big question. And the big question would only be permitted as a small parenthesis in the middle of the small question.

I happened lately to have a small debate with a very distinguished modern writer, Mr. Middleton Murry, on a book that he has written about Communism. I only mention it here because I soon discovered that I was not arguing against Communism but against Fatalism. I will not discuss the social and economic thesis, because, in truth, Mr. Middleton Murry's sort of Communism is rather a curious sort of Communism, which he alone would have the spirit and originality to explain. I do not agree with Communism; but I do not disagree with it because it would break up the existing system of commercialism. That, I think, is breaking itself up without any assistance from anybody. I disagree with Communism because I think it involves the sacrifice of Liberty. And the curious thing is that Mr. Middleton Murry does distinctly admit, in so many words, that it would involve the sacrifice of Liberty. So that he and I are so far in a state of blissful agreement; not practical agreement, but real or theoretical agreement. It is true that he adds to this a mystical paradox about losing freedom in order to be free, but he would

have to explain that for himself. Where I found myself in much more fundamental disagreement with him
was in this very ancient business about Fate; or, as he
prefers to call it, Necessity. God forbid that we should
go once more into the trampled labyrinth of Fate and
Freewill. It is enough for me that the second is at least
as fundamental an idea as the first; and really a more
fundamental idea than the first. It is quite certain that
I *feel* as if I could leave off writing this essay whenever
I like. Nobody can prove that feeling to be an illusion,
except by a universal scepticism which might equally
hold fate to be an illusion, or even law to be an illusion.
The Determinists of my youth used to boast that Science supported them, because some scientists talked
about the Determinism of Matter. I do not know what
they are saying now, when several scientists are actually talking about the Indeterminism of Matter. But,
anyhow, the idea of choice is an absolute, and nobody
can get behind it.

What interests me here especially is this. It seems
that many, who do probably feel they have freedom of
action in the present or in the future, are ready to talk
in a fatalistic way about the past. Mr. Middleton Murry,
though fatalistic in a general way, is especially fatalistic about the past. He repeats again and again that
whatever did happen was "necessary." He seems to

think it proved its necessity merely by happening. Now, I do not feel this about the past, any more than about the future. I admit necessity, in the sense of logical necessity. I admit that if I am heavier than Mr. Middleton Murry, it is necessary that Mr. Middleton Murry is lighter than I am. I admit that if three feet make a yard, it is necessary that six feet make two yards. In that sense I must concede that if (physically) six Murrys make one Chesterton and even (spiritually) six Chestertons make one Murry, any further calculations about the multiplication of these persons must be founded on the principles of the multiplication table. But I do not feel in the least as if it had been inevitable that I should have turned from an art student to a journalist; or inevitable that Mr. Murry should have turned to Bolshevism; or inevitable that Bolshevism should have ever turned up at all. In every historical event I feel the thrill of uncertainty and the suspense of the human choice, and I cannot understand why my feeling is not as reasonable as his feeling; which seems also to be a feeling and no more.

For what I really complain of in this brilliant and ingenious writer is that, whenever he does try to give ultimate reasons for his fixed fatalism and materialism, and consequent denial of miracle, he lets me down. I well remember how I came down with a crash, in the middle of the most exalted speculations, when he actually said he could not believe in something as a man "of the twentieth century." I know there are people who talk like that, but I had not classed him among them. I thought I was high up in the air arguing with Aristotle and Abelard, with Buddha and Spinoza, with Pythagoras or Confucius; and I came to earth with a bump, opposite a man who wanted to be known by a number. Can anybody imagine Spinoza presenting his cosmos as specially fitted to the eighteenth century? Would Abelard base his argument on the twelfth century, as the other on the twentieth century? Would even Confucius say that truth and wisdom must be reconciled with the requirements of his own particular date previous to the Han Dynasty? So far from saying this in disparagement of the writer's work as a whole, I remark on it as an incongruous interruption in his work as a whole. It seems to me that a number of these twentieth-century writers rebel not too much, but not half enough, against the nineteenth-century conventions. One of the Victorian conventions was that all was for the best, or at any rate that all was as it had to be. The Victorians were all convinced that William the Conqueror was bound to conquer; that Wellington was bound to beat Napoleon; that Canada was bound to cleave to England; that America was bound to cut herself off from England. And it seems to me that the mechanical optimism of Marx, and the necessitarian notion of history in moderns like Mr. Murry, is but a continuation in that optimistic groove. To me all the past is alive with alternatives, and nobody can show, nobody has really attempted to show, that they were not real alternatives. I think it quite possible that if Harold's northern campaign had been a week earlier, William the Norman's southern campaign might have been launched too late; that if Napoleon had decided, after his hesitation, to throw in the Old Guard at Borodino, there would have been no Moscow and no Waterloo; that there was a time when a few wise words might have saved the American Colonies or a few foolish words lost Canada; and so on. In short, I believe that, again and again, man was at the cross-roads and might have taken another road. Nobody can prove or disprove it metaphysically; but I am the more content with a philosophy which permits of occasional miracles, because the alternative philosophy does not even permit of alternatives. It forbids a man even to dream of anything so natural as the Ifs of History.

THE disadvantage of men not knowing the past is that they do not know the present. History is a hill or high point of vantage, from which alone men see the town in which they live or the age in which they are living. Without some such contrast or comparison, without some such shifting of the point of view, we should see nothing whatever of our own social surroundings. We should take them for granted, as the only possible social surroundings. We should be as unconscious of them as we are, for the most part, of the hair growing on our heads or the air passing through our lungs. It is the variety of the human story that brings out sharply the last turn that the road has taken, and it is the view under the arch of the gateway which tells us that we are entering a town.

Yet this sense of the past is curiously patchy among the most intelligent and instructed people, especially in modern England. Among a hundred such scraps and snippets, I saw this morning a literary competition in an exceedingly highbrow weekly, a prize being awarded for a conversation between a modern interviewer and St. George. And I was struck by the fact that clever, and even brilliant, contributors missed much of the point, even about the modern interviewer, by missing the point about the ancient saint. I am not setting up as an authority on either. I am not pretending to be learned; nor is there here any question of learning. It is a question of quite superficial information, but of information that is fairly well spread over the whole surface. I have not been right slap-bang through *The Decline and Fall of the Roman Empire* lately, any more than had Mr. Silas Wegg; I have not read every word of the *Acta Sanctorum* within the last week or so; I have not even read very closely the relatively modern romance of *The Seven Champions of Christendom*. I have nothing but general information; but it is fairly general. What surprises me in people younger, brighter, and more progressively educated than myself is that their general information is very patchy.

Now, it is unfair to say that they know nothing about St. George, because it may fairly be answered that there is nothing to be known about St. George. In one sense, nobody knows who St. George was; we only know who he was not. The only clear and solid fact about him is that he certainly was *not* what Gibbon said he was; the contractor of Cappadocia. He was merely recorded as a common soldier of the legions martyred with multitudes under Diocletian; nor is there any particular reason to doubt that he was. All the rest is legend, though legend is often very valuable to history. And I mean by general information the sense of the life in legends; how they grow; where they come from; why they remain. I know what saints were supposed to be; what patron saints were supposed to do; how they often did it for the most diverse groups ages after their death; how other saints besides George dealt with dragons; how other nations besides England invoked St. George; how the saints were before the knights; how the knights were before the nations; and so on. In short, I have picked up quite crudely what Mr. Wells calls an Outline of History; but a more scientifically educated generation still seems to have only snippets of history: the lie out of Gibbon; the legend about the dragon; the phrase "St. George for Merry England," and such isolated items. The result is a curious sort of narrowness, even about the problem of the present or the immediate past. For instance, one quite intelligent contributor apparently identified "St. George" as somebody supposed to have lived in "Merry England," and explained that his period (whatever it was supposed to be) was not really merry, because there was a great deal of mud in the streets, or people lived in mud hovels. Apart from everything else, I call it narrow for a man to suppose that Mud is the opposite of Merriment. Did he never make any mud-pies? Was he not much merrier making them than contributing to intellectual weeklies?

But the essential point is this. Everybody thought the joke must be found in showing how unlike St. George's time was to ours. I think it would be a much better joke to show how extremely like St. George's time was to ours. But the writers are hampered in this by being extremely vague about what was St. George's time. Now, a man in the later Roman Empire, like George the Martyr, would have seen all round him an ancient world that was astonishingly like the modern world. Whether or no Merry England was a suitable phrase for mediæval-ism, whether or no mediævalism was all mud, it is quite certain that the Empire of Diocletian was not all mud. Imperial Rome was not all mud, but all marble, all mortar and massive building, all pipes and tanks and engineering, all sorts of elaborate equipments of luxury or hygiene. And among all those palatial baths and towering aqueducts, George would probably be thinking pretty much what many an intelligent man is thinking now—that man does not live by soap alone; and that hygiene, or even health, is not much good unless you can take a healthy view of it—or, better still, feel a healthy indifference to it.

Suppose, for instance, that the soldier George had read

some of the satires on fashionable society that were produced in that old Pagan world. He would find fact after fact and fashion after fashion exactly parallel to our own. He would find Juvenal making fun of fashionable ladies who join in masculine sports or adventures in a spirit of self-advertisement. The Roman satirist describes how grand Roman ladies would appear as gladiators in the arena, sacrificing not only modesty, but the manners of their rank, in order to be in the limelight. That exact fashionable blend of Feminism and Publicity did really exist in the real epoch of the real St. George: almost exactly as it exists today. Or suppose the Roman soldier read the religious and philosophical literature circulating through the Roman Empire. He would find all that we call New Religions now already called New Religions then. He would find idealists who were Vegetarians, like Apollonius of Tyana; theosophists who had learned all about Reincarnation from Brahmins and Hindu seers; prophets of the Simple Life in the drawing-rooms of duchesses, talking about the secrets of health, wealth, and wisdom; promises of a new Universal Religion, which should include all beliefs without any particular belief in any of them. If the real original St. George did find himself interviewed by a modern newspaper man, he would think that hardly anything in the newspaper was new. He would not think primarily that he had come into a strange world, for away from dragons and princesses and mediæval armour. He would think he had got back into the old bewildered and decaying world of the last phase of Paganism, loud with denials of religion and louder with the howlings of superstition. He would find everything in Juvenal—except Juvenal. He would find quite as many absurd lady gladiators— only not so many people calling them absurd. He would be quite at home, thinking himself back in the old Diocletian Empire—and he would prepare for death.

THERE appears at regular intervals in the Sunday Press, like the article on the Cuckoo or Christmas Shopping, an article on the supposed superstition of the Good Old Times, laboriously alleging that they were really Bad Old Times. This article appeared in due course, in a popular weekly, under the title of "What is Right with the World"; but, except for the title, the article was the same. The same examples, the same hackneyed historical details, the same comfortable moral in almost exactly the same words. There are several things that are rather curious about this well-known journalistic feature. One is that the article professes to be an answer to another article which does not exist. I have never in my life seen the first original offending statement, that the Good Old Times really were Good Old Times. I have never heard any rational human being talking about the Good Old Times. I have heard a great many rational and highly intellectual and instructed people talking about the advantages of certain particular institutions that existed at certain particular periods. Thus I have heard political economists of the first rank saying that the Apprentice-

ship System was the best training for trades and the
world would be wise to return to it. Or I have heard
historians of high authority say that it was easier to
create international understanding and peace in the days
when all the nations knew Latin . . . and pronounced
it in the same way. I have heard very modern experts
wish there were more people back on the land, and regret that for a hundred years they had poured into the
overcrowded towns. I have even listened to daring
thinkers who thought our position was more financially
regular before we went off the Gold Standard; who
positively regretted the process of lowering wages in
order to start businesses; who would have it that our big
industries were better off when they lived on a profit
and not on an overdraft, and who stuck to their old
paradox that banking was safer when there were not
so many banks going bust. In short, I have known many
perverse persons who held that, in this or that particular
respect, we were better off in this or that particular
period. But this visionary man who walks about the
streets in funereal garb, wailing aloud, and at large over
the disappearance of some undefined and undated Good
Old Days—I have never met him, I rather doubt
whether anybody has ever met him; and I doubt still
more whether it is necessary to reprint the same article
so many hundreds of times in order to check his pes-

tilential influence.

The second curious thing about the article is this: that, though it is always introduced in the very vaguest terms, it always does gravitate eventually in the direction of one particular period, and it is always practically the same period. It is always, I may add, the very worst period that could possibly be chosen, for any purpose of practical comparison. It is (as in the present example) the period of about a hundred and fifty years ago. It is a very bad selection, because that date does not mark any other or older system; it only marks the most crude and clumsy beginnings of our present or modern system. It is not like saying that there was another world, for better or worse, before Rousseau or before Luther or before Christ, in the ancient Pagan world. At the date chosen we already had machinery, but much cruder machinery; we already had big towns, but much more unfinished and disorderly big towns; we already had a complete dependence on commerce, but as yet on a much more cut-throat competitive commerce. It is naturally not difficult to show that we are better than our great-grandfathers, when we are doing in a finished way what they were also doing, but in an unfinished way. The only question is whether, in another sense, we are not something that they most certainly were not: and that is, finished.

Everyone knows the list of examples. Our fathers hanged men for petty thefts, whereas we only exalt and ennoble men or put them in the House of Lords for really large and impressive thefts. But I am not troubled here by such questions, but only by the sameness and the lack of any lively curiosity about questions on the other side. Thus it begins with drunkenness; how typical of that type of moralist to begin with drunkenness . . . as if nothing else could be quite so immoral! "In those days there was undoubtedly more drunkenness." I wonder. There was certainly more drunkenness among those who could stand it best; strong men who rode hard in country air and drank before they slept. Was there more drunkenness among schoolgirls than there is in America, or more drunkenness among Society girls than there now is in Mayfair? I wonder. But I wonder, most of all, why this sort of questioner is always content with his one fixed question. Suppose I were to ask him a question. Does he think there was a bigger trade in cocaine and drugs before the Battle of Waterloo than there is now?

After mentioning the one really dreadful thing, which is drunkenness, the writer goes on more vaguely about brutality and ignorance and injustice and the rest. It is difficult to test these things, because there are different moral standards in different people and different periods. For instance, I think it is just that every man should be a free owner of primary property, like land and tools. I therefore think a just commonwealth will have a multitude of peasant proprietors and small shopkeepers. The writer must know, if he knows anything, that these small men were steadily disappearing—or rather, being destroyed—all through what he considers the great period of progress. I do not say there were not other things in which our forefathers were unjust. I only wonder, by this time somewhat wearily, why the story of the Yeoman never even occurs to the writers of the perennial article.

Then the writer gives an astonishing example. "The press-gang was still a favourite method of recruiting members for His Majesty's Army or Navy." The press-gang was a black blot on Britain; a thoroughly mean piece of brutality; but why? Because until then it was universally held that English fighters were all volunteers and enlisted freely. The press-gang was a piece of illegal and treacherous Conscription, used by men who were ashamed to use legal and universal Conscription. But the men of the modern world are not ashamed to use legal and universal Conscription. All the enlightened modern States used it in the last war, and they will use it more in the next war. It is a specially and particularly modern thing. In short, a gigantic Press-Gang, crimping and crushing not somebody but everybody, is one of the most towering and typical creations of the last hundred and fifty years.

That is what I complain of in this sort of regular journalistic philosophy. Not that it criticizes conditions a hundred years ago, when there were, heaven knows, plenty of things to criticize. But that it is intellectually incapable of criticizing conditions now, when there are new and different things to criticize. Nobody can take in the scale of the modern changes, let alone feel free enough of them to note what is sinister or dubious about them. For instance, nobody has yet measured the meaning of State education, with its practical elimination of the parent; at least of the poor parent. In a real study of modern and relatively recent things it would be necessary to go into these questions. But if somebody merely says that my grandfather used candles and I use electric light, I am content to answer that when I was in the most modern American hotels, it was the very latest fashion to lower all the electric lights till they gave rather less light than a candle.

It grows plainer, every day, that those of us who cling to crumbling creeds and dogmas, and defend the dying traditions of the Dark Ages, will soon be left alone defending the most obviously decaying of all those ancient dogmas: the idea called Democracy. It has taken not quite a lifetime, roughly my own lifetime, to bring it from the top of its success, or alleged success, to the bottom of its failure, or reputed failure. By the end of the nineteenth century, millions of men were accepting democracy without knowing why. By the end of the twentieth century, it looks as if millions of people will be rejecting democracy, also without knowing why. In such a straight, strictly logical and unwavering line does the Mind of Man advance along the great Path of Progress.

Anyhow, at the moment, democracy is not only being abused, but being very unfairly abused. Men are blaming universal suffrage, merely because they are not enlightened enough to blame original sin. There is one simple test for deciding whether popular political evils are due to original sin. And that is to do what none or very few of these modern malcontents are doing; to state any sort of moral claim for any other sort of political system. The essence of democracy is very simple and, as Jefferson said, self-evident. If ten men are wrecked together on a desert island, the community consists of those ten men, their welfare is the social object, and normally their will is the social law. If they have not a natural claim to rule themselves, which of them has a natural claim to rule the rest? To say that the cleverest or boldest will rule is to beg the moral question. If his talents are used for the community, in planning voyages or distilling water, then he is the servant of the community; which is, in that sense, his sovereign. If his talents are used against the community, by stealing rum or poisoning water, why should the community submit to him? and is it in the least likely that it will? In such a simple case as that, everybody can see the popular basis of the thing, and the advantage of government by consent. The trouble with democracy is that it has never, in modern times, had to do with such a simple case as that. In other words, the trouble with democracy is not democracy. It is certain artificial anti-democratic things that have, in fact, thrust themselves into the modern world to thwart and destroy democracy.

Modernity is not democracy; machinery is not democracy; the surrender of everything to trade and commerce is not democracy. Capitalism is not democracy; and is admittedly, by trend and savour, rather against democracy. Plutocracy by definition is not democracy. But all these modern things forced themselves into the world at about the time, or shortly after the time, when great idealists like Rousseau and Jefferson happened to have been thinking about the democratic ideal of democracy. It is tenable that the ideal was too idealistic to succeed. It is not tenable that the ideal that failed was the same as the realities that did succeed. It is one thing to say that a fool went into a jungle and was devoured by wild beasts; it is quite another to say that he himself survives as the one and only wild beast. Democracy has had everything against it in practice, and that very fact may be something against it in theory. It may be argued that it has human life against it. But, at any rate, it is quite certain that it has modern life against it. The industrial and scientific world of the last hundred years has been much *more* unsuitable a setting for the experiment of self-government than would have been found in old conditions of agrarian or even nomadic life. Feudal manorial life was not a democracy; but it could have been much more easily turned into a democracy. Later peasant life, as in France or Switzerland, actually has been quite easily turned into a democracy. But it is horribly hard to turn what is called modern industrial democracy into a democracy.

That is why many men are now beginning to say that the democratic ideal is no longer in touch with the modern spirit. I strongly agree; and I naturally prefer the democratic ideal, which is at least an ideal, and therefore, an idea, to the modern spirit, which is simply modern and, therefore, already becoming ancient. I notice that the cranks, whom it would be more polite to call the idealists, are already hastening to shed this ideal. A well-known Pacifist, with whom I argued in Radical papers in my Radical days, and who then passed as a pattern Republican of the New Republic, went out of his way the other day to say, "The voice of the people is commonly the voice of Satan." The truth is that these Liberals never did really believe in popular government, any more than in anything else that was popular, such as public-houses or the Dublin Sweepstake. They did not believe in the democracy they invoked against kings and priests. But I did believe in it; and I do believe in it, though I much preferred to invoke it against prigs and faddists. I still believe it would be the most human sort of government, if it could be once more attempted in a more human time.

Unfortunately, humanitarianism has been the mark

of an inhuman time. And by inhumanity, I do not mean merely cruelty; I mean the condition in which even cruelty ceases to be human. I mean the condition in which the rich man, instead of hanging six or seven of his enemies because he hates them, merely beggars and starves to death six or seven thousand people whom he does not hate, and has never seen, because they live at the other side of the world. I mean the condition in which the courtier or pander of the rich man, instead of excitedly mixing a rare, original poison for the Borgias, or carving an exquisite ornamental poignard for the political purposes of the Medici, works monotonously in a factory turning out a small type of screw, which will fit into a plate he will never see; to form part of a gun he will never see; to be used in a battle he will never see, and about the merits of which he knows far less than the Renaissance rascal knew about the purposes of the poison and the dagger. In short, what is the matter with industrialism is indirection; the fact that nothing is straightforward; that all its ways are crooked even when they are meant to be straight. Into this most indirect of all systems we tried to fit the most direct of all ideas. Democracy, an ideal which is simple to excess, was vainly applied to a society which was complex to the point of craziness. It is not so very surprising that such a vision has faded in such an environment. Personally, I like the vision; but it takes all sorts to make a world, and there actually are human beings, walking about quite calmly in the daylight, who appear to like the environment.

A NEWSPAPER appeared with the news, which it seemed to regard as exciting and even alarming news, that Gray did not write the "Elegy in a Country Churchyard" in the churchyard of Stoke Poges, but in some other country churchyard of the same sort in the same country. What effect the news will have on the particular type of American tourist who has chipped pieces off trees and tombstones, when he finds that the chips come from the wrong trees, or the wrong tombstones, I do not feel impelled to inquire. Nor, indeed, do I know whether the new theory is proved or not. Nor do I care whether the new theory is proved or not. What is most certainly proved, if it needed any proving, is the complete lack of imagination, in many journalists and archæologists, about how any poet writes any poem.

In such a controversy it is implied, generally on both sides, that what happens is something like this. The poet comes and sits on a tombstone, or wherever he was supposed to sit, in the one and only churchyard of Stoke Poges, or whatever place be the rival of Stoke Poges. He hears the Curfew; and there is a dreadful doubt and dispute about whether anybody sitting among the tombs of Stoke Poges can hear the Curfew, which does really ring from Windsor, though I imagine it sounds pretty much like any other bell at evening. Then the poet produces a portable pen and ink, preferably a large quill and a scroll (the poet in question lived before the time of fountain-pens), and writes down the first line: "The curfew tolls the knell of parting day." Then he looks round to make quite sure that there are some lowing herds winding over that particular lea, that the ploughman is present and doing his duty in plodding homeward his weary way, and that all the other fittings are in the offing. Later, he will have to insist peremptorily on an ivy-mantled tower being in the immediate neighbourhood, inhabited by an (if possible) moping owl. It will not be the only owl involved in the business. If there are not all these correct conditions provided on the spot, he will not be able to write the Elegy. If, on the other hand, they are all there and everything has been properly provided, he will then write the whole of the Elegy, steadily, right through, and not roll up his scroll or rise from his tombstone until he has left the unfortunate young man in the poem finally safe in the bosom of his Father and his God. Then he will go home to tea; and I should imagine he would need it, after so prolonged and sustained a literary effort achieved in such damp and clammy conditions. That, with very little exaggeration, is what is really suggested by those who talk about Gray writing the poem in this place or that place, and under this or that condition of local colour.

Now, I should have thought that anybody would know that poetry is not written like that. But perhaps, in this case, even a bad poet is better than a good critic. Anybody who has ever written any verse, good, bad, or indifferent, will know that calculations of this sort are calculations about the incalculable. Gray might have written the poem, or any part of the poem, in any place on the map; he might have visited the New Stoke Poges or the Old Stoke Poges, or quite probably both, or possibly neither. But, if I may be allowed to pick out one thread of speculation from a thousand threads of possibility, I would suggest that the "Elegy in a Country Churchyard," even if it did refer to one particular churchyard, is very likely to have been begun, continued, and ended rather like this:

Mr. Thomas Gray was sitting one evening in a coffee-house; let us hope a coffee-house that did not confine itself to coffee. Something or other, a fiddle or a few glasses of wine, or a good dinner, had thrown him into a mood of musing, of pleasant musing, though touched with a manly and generous melancholy. His thoughts turned round and round, as they do at such times, the tantalizing old riddle of what we really feel about life and death; about the toy God gave us which is beautiful and brittle, yet certainly not trivial. He said to himself: "After all, who doesn't really feel that it really matters, with all its botherations? . . . A queer business . . . pleasing . . . anxious. . . ." Then something stirred quicker within him, and he said to himself, in warm poetic emotion—

> For who tytumpty tumpty tumpty tum,
> This pleasing anxious being e'er resigned.

Then his impulse gathered speed and power; and he struck the table and said the next line straight off—

> Left the warm precincts of the cheerful day.

He said that line several times. He liked it very much. Then it was almost a matter of form, certainly a matter of facility, to put the tail on the verse—

> Nor cast one longing, lingering look behind.

Then he got up and put on his hat. He left the warm precincts of the cheerful coffee-house, and went home and forgot all about it.

Some time afterwards, perhaps quite a long time afterwards, he was walking in the countryside at dusk. It is quite possible that he was walking in Stoke Poges, or through Stoke Poges, or through any number of other places in the neighbourhood. Perhaps he did hear the Curfew, or what he thought was the Curfew, or what he pretended was the Curfew. He made up another verse or two about the twilight landscape, full of the same spirit of stoical thankfulness and genial resignation. Then he noticed, with great joy, that they would work into the same metre as the lines he had made up in the coffee-house. They were very much in the same mood. But he did not write many of the verses in the church-yard. Possibly he did not write any of the verses in the churchyard. It is more likely that the third act has for its scene Mr. Gray's private study, lined with the classics in old leather bindings, and adorned with the celebrated cat and the bowl of goldfish. There he jotted down disjointed verses, and began to put them together; until it looked as if they might some day make a poem. But, subject to any information that may exist on the subject, it would not in the ordinary way surprise me to learn that it was a devil of a long time before they did make a poem. It is most likely, in the abstract, that he got sick of it half-way through, and chucked it away, and found it again years afterwards. It is extremely likely that there was another very long interval, when he was just finishing it, but could not finish finishing it. Many a man writing such a poem has held it up for a year for want of one verse. Nor would the newspaper assist him, in such a difficulty, by pointing out that there was another churchyard much more suitable than that of Stoke Poges.

Now, it is possible—nay, it is probable—that there is not one word of truth in this particular description of the proceedings of Mr. Gray. I have not read any of the literary and biographical records of Mr. Gray, at least for a long time; and there are plenty of records to read. It is quite likely that there are details of his daily life that destroy altogether the details I have here suggested. It is even possible that, by some amazing eccentricity, he did write the whole thing in a churchyard; or, by some unscrupulous exaggeration, pretended that he had done so. But my story is a great deal nearer to the normal story of the production of a poem than any story that supposes particular places and conditions to be *necessary* to the poem. Even if Gray did write with all the stage properties stuck up around him, the lowing cow, the plodding ploughman, the moping owl, they were not the materials of the poem; and he would probably have written pretty much the same sort of poem without them. All this business of clues and tests is not criticism. It is a very good thing that people are applying literature to detective stories and detectives. But it is not a

good thing to apply detectives to literature. Gray's un-
mistakable foot-mark or favourite tobacco-ash may be
found in Stoke Poges or anywhere else. But it is not in
those ashes that there lived his wonted fires.

The real relation of Gray's great poem to the present
stage of our history will probably not be understood
until a later stage. Yet the poem is a monument, a
trophy, and, at the same time, a beacon or signal, standing up as solid and significant as the monument stands
up in the Stoke Poges fields. Many poems have been
written since, and grown more fashionable, if not more
famous, which have not the particular meaning for the
modern world stored up in this very storied urn. For
Gray wrote at the very beginning of a certain literary
epoch of which we, perhaps, stand at the very end. He
represented that softening of the Classic which slowly
turned it into the Romantic. We represent that ultimate
hardening of the Romantic which has turned it into the
Realistic. Both changes have, of course, been criticized
in their time by the more conservative critics. Dr. Johnson said, probably with a partly humorous impatience,
that Gray had only proved that he "could be dull in a
new way." And most of us will agree that the modern
realistic writers, who have in their turn replaced the
romantic writers, have indubitably discovered a marvel-
lous and amazing number of new ways of being dull.

But the change, as it hung uncompleted in Gray, strangely resembled the twilight changes of that landscape which the poem describes. Indeed, the whole episode has a curious, almost uncanny, harmony that even includes coincidence. Concerned as he was with a fine shade of twilight, it is even odd that his name was Gray. The whole legend is like that of something colourless and classical fading into mere shadow. For something was, indeed, fading before the eyes of Thomas Gray, the poet, and it was something that he did not wish to see fade. It may be noted that the first impression, especially in the first verses, is one of things moving away from the poet and leaving him alone. We see only the back of the ploughman, so to speak, as he plods away into the darkness; the herds of cattle have the perspective of vanishing things; for a whole world was indeed passing out of the sight and reach of that learned and sensitive and secluded gentleman, who represented the culture of eighteenth-century England, and could only watch a twilight transformation which he could not understand. For when the ploughman comes back out of that twilight, he will come back different. He will be either a scientific works-manager or an entirely new kind of agrarian citizen, great as in the first days of Rome; a free peasant or a servant of alien machinery; but never the same again.

I am not very fond of committees and societies of specialists or amateurs who sit upon this or that sort of problem; but in the particular problem of the preservation of the rural and cultural traditions of our own countryside, I cannot see at the moment that any other machinery is possible. And it seems to me that the Penn-Gray Society is a good example of a machine suited to its work and doing work that is wanted. The trouble is that the typical cultured Englishman, like Gray or the traditional admirer of Gray, was generally a certain kind of gentleman, of the sort that had some kind of country seat. Since then, to continue the figure, the gentleman with the country seat has rather fallen between two stools. He is no longer so rich and powerful as a landlord. He generally has not become rich and powerful as a local politician. There were any number of men, of course, who appreciated the country without owning a country seat. But if they were not the sort of men to own a country seat, still less were they the sort of men to stand for a county council. And, as the old organization of England went, the organization that has been gradually dying since the days of Gray, men of this artistic sort were mostly attached in some more or less indirect way to the gentry. That is the point; that, for good or ill, it was the system peculiar to a gentry. It was never, for instance, the system peculiar to a peasantry. When there is anything like a peasantry, even as there is in Scotland, it was possible to produce a peasant poet like Burns. And the memory of a peasant like Burns would be preserved by other peasants, even if there were nobody else to preserve it. But nobody could expect the agricultural labourers to preserve the memory of a scholar like Gray. It is amusing to remember that Burns put a verse from the Elegy as a motto to his own homely and pungent picture of peasant life; as some have thought, consciously stressing the contrast between his own realism and the scholar's classicism:

> Let not ambition mock their useful toil,
>   Their humble joys, and destiny obscure;
> Nor grandeur hear, with a disdainful smile,
>   The short and simple annals of the poor.

Indeed, I rather fancy that, in citing those rather patronizing lines, it was the poor poet who had the disdainful smile.

But we must take the rough with the smooth in that noble aristocratic story that has made South England like a garden among the nations. And with it weakened the only organization for protecting the art and antiquities of rural life. Gray could not be a popular poet like Burns; at least, not in that sort of rural life. Perhaps there is a hint of it in his own phrase; that the Village Milton would have remained mute and inglorious. Perhaps he deliberately did not finish the tale of the Village Hampden, who was possibly a poacher, but could not possibly be a peasant. Anyhow, the old organization of culture has weakened; and the new organization of local politics is not an organization of culture. There can be a culture of peasants, but not a culture of petty politicians. In this dilemma there is nothing to be done except to work through groups of sympathetic individuals, students or artists or lovers of landscape, who take the trouble to support each other in defending the tradition of the national history and poetry. Otherwise the whole country will be swept bare for the sort of motorist to whom every object is an obstacle to rushing from nowhere to nowhere. Roads will not be roads, for there will be no places for them to go to; there will be only those ominously called arterial, and resembling, indeed, those open and spouting arteries that are an inevitable sign of death. I should say the ultimate moral is that we ought to have made up our minds between real aristocracy and real democracy, and should have either preserved a gentry or created a peasantry. But the immediate moral is that we must preserve what we can of all that reminds us that rural life was a civilization and not a savagery, and especially support such groups as the society here in question, which is defending the great tradition of Gray.

WITH the high priests of Mumbo-Jumbo I am on friendly terms; with the worshippers of the Green Monkey and the Seven-headed Snake I can chat cheerfully if we meet by chance in society; with the Blood-drinkers of Baphomet I have tactfully agreed to differ; with the Howling Dervishes of the Red Desert I see the road open to reunion; from those who offer their babies to the Most Ancient Crocodile I differ only in opinion; of those who consider it a sign of divine favour that their mother's head is bitten off by a Bengal tiger, I am willing to believe that they are better than their creed; to those who believe the sea to be the green blood of a great giant whose anæmic visage is exhibited in the moon, I am ready to concede that we may be looking at two different aspects of truth; in those who sincerely hope to gratify the god of their fathers by eating nothing but live scorpions, I respectfully salute a counsel of perfection which I am not myself called upon to follow; in those who paint themselves scarlet all over and dance before the Nine-headed Elephant, I recognize a ritualistic practice which franker and fuller discussion might well commend even to less advanced schools of thought in the Universal Church; of Thugs I think hopefully; of Bashi-Bazouks I hear the most reassuring news; and to Christian Scientists I extend Christian charity. But there is one way of writing about such things and such people which seems to me to suggest something utterly sub-human and much less than half-witted; something so stunted that we can hardly recognize it as the stature of manhood; something so stupid that we can hardly call it the mind of man; something so flat and unlifting that it might possibly be the mind of one of those flat, pale fishes that lie on the floor of the deep dark sea and live only in two dimensions. And this mentality is the mentality of a large number of people who write educational works on evolutionary history, and are so grossly benighted that they really believe themselves to be enlightened.

For the depths of a superstition, even the depths of a degradation, are at least depths. They do not shout with shallow conceit at finding nothing but shallows. There is something in the grossest idolatry or the craziest mythology that has a quality of groping and adumbration. There is more in life than we understand; some have told us that if we ate a scorpion or worshipped a green monkey we might understand it better. But the evolutionary educator, having never since his birth been in anything but the dark, naturally believes that he is in the daylight. His very notion of daylight is something which is so blank as to be merely blind. There are no depths in it, either of light or darkness. There are no dimensions in it; not only no fourth, but no third, no second, and hardly a first; certainly no dimensions in which the mind can move. Therefore the mind remains fixed, in a posture that is called progressive. It never looks back, even for remembrance; it never looks the other way, even for experiment; it never looks at the other side, even for a paradox; it never winks the other eye. It simply knows all there is; and there does not seem to be much to know. I have recently been looking through a specimen of this sort of scientific summary of the story of man; and I am relieving my feelings.

Those writers sometimes say they are agnostic about God. Would to God they would consent to be agnostics about Man! Would they would leave the love of beauty or mystery as mysterious as they really are. Every child is born facing some open questions. He finds them open just as he finds his ears or his lungs or his nostrils open; and he knows by instinct that through these open questions he draws in the air and life of the universe. Why dreams are different from daylight, why dead things are different from live things, why he himself is different from others, why beauty makes us restless and even love is a spring of quarrels, why we cannot so fit into our environment as to forget it and ourselves; all these things are felt vaguely by children on long, empty afternoons; or by primitive poets writing the epics and legends of the morning of the world. And all legends, however barbaric, are filled with the wind of all this wider questioning. They all refer back to these ancient unfathomable wells which go down deeper than the reason into the very roots of the world, but contain the springs that refresh the reason and keep it active for ever. The object of the rationalist historian is to choke up those wells. He puts in a sort of plug, like a stupid plumber, to stop the flowing of the fountain of youth. The plug is generally a word; a stupid word used as a stopper upon thought. It does not solve the mystery; it only stupefies or paralyses the power to realize that it is a mystery. When a boy wants to walk about, he knows it is mixed up with feelings he has not fathomed and a song called "Over the Hills and Far Away." When a poet walks about, he realizes something strange in the fact that he can walk about, and that a tree or a mountain cannot walk about. But the object of the pseudo-scientist is to utter a sort of formula of enchantment which will chill and freeze these wanderers for ever. If their bodies still move about, at least their minds will never move again.

He utters the magic words "Man has evolved powers of locomotion"; and man loses them on the spot. Those who were previously walking about remain stuck like statues in the garden of the wizard.

To take one case: the book I read repeated for the millionth time that modesty must be meaningless because the amount of clothing varies among various races. As if any theologian or moralist of standing ever said that the divine plan of the universe dictated a particular length of skirt! All they dictated was decent acquiescence in whatever was regarded as a reasonably unobtrusive length of skirt. But the writer did not think much of modesty as a reason for clothing; it was mentioned in Genesis and therefore could not be true. Now it is quite true that ornament is a very early element in this mysterious human behaviour; though the ornament often refers to taboos about sex. But this writer could not be content to say that dress began with ornament. He must insist on saying that dress began with ostentation. That is to say, he was bound to begin with a word that belittles and depreciates; even when it is inapplicable. A whole tribe could not wear the same clothes out of ostentation; and in our modern tribe it is commoner to wear no clothes with that object. Besides, ornament began with all sorts of things other than clothes; pottery and walls and weapons and so on.

And if the writer supposes that one superior baboon could say to another slightly inferior baboon, "Paint or weave me an ornament that coils like the whirlpool or dances like the waves, that catches the stars in a net or branches into suns like a rose-tree into roses; because I am feeling ostentatious this morning," and that the common workman would then carry out the task—why then the writer considerably underrates the subtlety even of the most primitive and prehistoric art. But he must have a word that shrivels and cheapens something; so he calls the whole mystery of the human thirst for beauty "ostentation." But anybody, who has read many books of this swaggering scientific sort, knows that there can be a good deal of ostentation with no beauty at all.

ALMOST immediately after the end of the Great War a German wrote a highly successful or widely boomed book called *The Decline of the West*. The most human inference (in the opinion of many) was that the German, having assisted at the spectacle of the Decline and Fall of the German Empire, naturally wanted all the rest of us to decline and fall with him. He felt it would be obviously a breach of taste and tact for any nation to flourish if Germany had declined; if, indeed, he was even aware of the existence of such fringes of his Empire as France or Flanders or England. Anyhow, he applied his doctrine to all that is most active in our civilization, whether we are so constituted as to call it the Indo-Germanic race or prefer to call it Christendom. But there was more in this theory of his about a general collapse; which was also a theory of a recurrent collapse. In this, indeed, and in his general idea of a modern phase of decline, his view was quite reasonable and very persuasively stated. But there was bound up with it another set of ideas which are not necessarily any part of the theory, either that civilizations periodically weaken or that our civilization has weakened in our period. Those two theses may quite well be true; but the thesis of the book was false.

For me, at least, it was false because it was fatalist; false because it was unhistoric; and false because it involved a particular falsity about the very spirit of the great culture which the critic criticized. It is the whole point of that culture that it has been continuous; it was the whole point of the critic that it had been discontinuous and disconnected. He was not content to say that civilizations revolve in separate cycles, in the sense in which we might be said to belong to a different civilization from the Druids. He cut up ordinary European history into chunks, that were supposed to have no more to do with each other than Chinese history and Aztec history. He chopped ordinary Christian history in two in the middle, in order to deny that either part of it was Christian. So far as I remember, he attributed the first half of it entirely to the Moslem Arabs, because they were not Christians; and the second half of it to people of the type of Faust, because they were rather fishy sort of Christians, and German as well. And he talked about these divisions as if they were like the abysses that might separate a stratum full of primordial crystals from a stratum, æons afterwards, containing the first fantastic traces of marsupial life.

Now, I am quite certain, as a matter of mere common sense, that the history of Christendom, or even the history of Europe, was never so fragmentary as that. We are much more connected with the ancient Greeks than the German writer would allow us to be with the later mediævals, or even the earlier moderns. The sort of distinction he suggested only happens when a cycle of civilization really dies, and then fossilizes and remains as inscrutable as an ammonite. We have no idea what was the religion of the Cro-Magnans, though we infer from certain pictures of ritual dances (as well as from our own common sense) that they had one. We do not know the significance of the Cup and Ring Stones, though the fortunate and civilized of us still use rings, as in the case of wedding-rings, or cups even in the sense of wine-cups. We do not even know if we interpret the signs rightly, or whether they are signs at all. Now, the Greek gods have never died in that fashion; and the Roman Empire has never died at all. Of the most modern industrial cities in England, many have in their very names the title of the Roman Camp; and wherever there stood the Roman Camp, there stood afterwards the Christian Cathedral. There was never one moment, in the long history from Herodotus to Herr Spengler, when all the men who counted in any age did not talk of The Fall of Troy; there was never a generation when young poets did not make that old tale a topic for new poems. I wonder whether a poem by Heredia about Antony, or a poem by Morris about Arthur, belongs to the dead Greek period or the dead Arabic period? There was never a generation when poets did not invoke Virgil, if only to imitate him. There was never a generation in which philosophers did not refer to Aristotle, if only to contradict him. The thread of our cultural continuity has never been broken.

I think the fact worth recording at the moment for two reasons. The first is that the same energetic German author has launched yet another book, of much less dignity and of much more dogmatism, reaffirming his theory, and especially the most gloomy and barbaric parts of it. The other is that there is a horrible possibility that what he says falsely about our past may be said truly about our present and our future. I mean that, hitherto, the men of our ancient tradition have done everything except forget. Whatever might be fanatical or ill-balanced about their religions or their revolutions, they have each, in turn, taken particular care to remember the deeds of their fathers. Even when they poisoned the purer Paganism of Homer and Pindar, they did not destroy it; they left it standing for ever against them as a reproach. Even when they dethroned the Greek gods they did not dismiss them; in the first just fury they denounced them as devils, but in the long run they let them remain as elves. They let them remain as fanciful and fabulous figures, for literary metaphor or plastic decoration, so that Christendom has left the nymph in poetry or the cupid in sculpture. It is true that now, for the first time, the race that has always remembered is invited on every side to forget.

Yes; it is true that today, for the first time, our newspapers and our new politicians have asked us to forget, not what happened a thousand years ago or a hundred years ago, but what happened twenty years ago. When it is a question of shifting a policy or rehabilitating a politician, they will ask us to forget what happened two years ago or two months ago. Here, indeed, we have the great Spengler System, of total separation of one historical episode from another. Here is the true trick of regarding ourselves as divided by æons and abysses, not only from our fathers, but from ourselves. Thus, by reading the daily paper every day, and forgetting everything that it said on the previous day, we can divide human history into self-contained cycles; each consisting, not of five hundred years, but of twenty-four hours. By this means we can regard the politician we trusted last week as we regard the cave-man whose carvings we could not decipher in a hundred years. By this means we can consider the slogans and swaggering policies which we ourselves cheered only recently, as if they were hieroglyphics as unintelligible as the Cup and Ring Stones. This new quality of forgetfulness, in our current culture, does give some justification to the pessimism of the German professor; and if we accept such oblivion, then doubtless our "cycle" will really curl up like a worm on the floor and lie still for ever.

Mr. Arthur Bryant recently published, through
Messrs. Longmans, a very thoughtful and interesting
study of King Charles II. It was certainly a favourable
portrait; but it was a portrait, and not an effigy or an
idol or a whitewashed statue, any more than a caricature.
There is room for difference of opinion about the propor-
tions of the picture, but it was a picture of a real object.
It has been the curse of our waxwork history that to each
historical figure was attached some more or less legendary
saying like a label, and even when the saying was partly
true it always missed the point of the truth. The point,
the peculiar truth, about Charles II always seems to me
to be this—that he was an amazing coincidence. He
was a prince born to inherit a crown; and he was an
extremely able man and, on a lower level, a sort of
genius. The label, or literary allusion, officially attached
to Charles II is almost always that epigram by one of
his intimates to the effect that he "never said a foolish
thing and never did a wise one." But indeed it was the
epigrammatist who said the foolish thing. It was, in
reality, nearly the reverse of the truth. Charles II, being

a man who had maintained fashionable light conversation down to his very deathbed, being, moreover, a man who must have made love to about forty women, must surely have gone to his grave having said a very large number of foolish things. But he had also done a very large number of wise things; and some things which a critic might well criticize as too wise, as having rather the wisdom of the serpent than the harmlessness of the dove. Indeed, I cannot recall at the moment that he ever did a thing that was unwise, though on some occasions he may have done a thing that was unworthy. Mr. Belloc, in his book on James II, has in some sense emphasized this aspect. He has in some sense set James II against Charles II; the former as the thoroughly sincere man who always has the appearance of being stupid and stubborn, the latter as the complex, compromising, and less heroic man who always seems to be tactful and reasonable. Mr. Arthur Bryant's version might almost be called a defence of Charles II against this implied comparison. He has no difficulty in showing that Charles was in a desperately difficult position, that the main fault lay with the fools, frauds, and bigots who pressed upon him; but I am not sure whether he entirely disposes of the appeal to the heroic made by Mr. Belloc, who wrote: "If he had resisted, he would have lost his Crown? He should have resisted and lost his Crown.

For there are other things that a man may lose."

But, whatever we may think of the man's moral quality, I am still surprised that nobody has taken anything like adequate notice of his mental quality. None of the Stuarts was stupid, in the sense that the term might be applied to the first German Georges. Mary Queen of Scots was brilliant and accomplished; James I was a learned man; Charles I was a cultivated man; James II was a capable man, especially as an administrator of the Navy; and whatever be the truth about the rather dim and dismal figure of the First Pretender, it is obvious that Charles Edward of the '45 was a fighter and no fool. But it seems to me that Charles II stands out from the Stuarts in really having the sort of brain that might have brought him into prominence if he had not been a prince. Much of the mistake arises from the blind and blundering trick of talking as if that sort of man were merely a "wit," and talking as if "wit" were only a sort of silly spangle or tinsel ornament that any fool could flaunt. In fact, there is much more wisdom in the old use of the word "wit" than in the new. In the old phrases about a man setting his wits to work, or having wit enough to do this or that, the word was really used as a synonym for mind. It does almost always stand for mind, but especially for presence of mind. Many, who quote the cheeky courtier's carefully prepared couplet about never saying a foolish thing and never doing a wise one do not mention Charles's much more piercing and quite impromptu reply to it, in that passage in which he is reported as answering: "I am an English King; and my words are my own, but my actions are my Ministers'." The man who talked like that did not merely have wit, or what these people mean by wit; he had brains.

Now, if we read the detailed, dramatic, and thrilling account, in Mr. Bryant's book, of Charles II's long game of political Poker against the politicians of the Opposition, really brilliant men like Shaftesbury and Halifax, we shall be watching a pure battle of brains, in which his brains were certainly the best. He, began with no cards at all; at least, he never had anything but bad cards in the worst time of the battle; he had all the ablest men of the age holding all the cards of the game against him; and he beat them all. He weathered a Revolution; which is only not classed with the Glorious Revolution or the American Revolution because he weathered it. And James II and George III did not. And he achieved a Restoration; not as a young prince coming back by the chance of birth or the choice of Parliament, but as an old, weary, and entirely lonely politician, in spite of Parliament, and by sheer unflagging intelligence. For the Restoration did not happen at the beginning of Charles's reign, but at the end.

It would be difficult to decide here on the merits of his cause, on which men will differ according to their religious and political partialities. It is well to note, however, that here again most people who discuss the politics miss the point. Thus they often read into the factions and fanaticisms of the period a modern democratic ideal that did not then exist either in the Whigs or in the King, but, if anything, rather more in the King than in the Whigs. When, for instance, Charles said that he thought his people would rather have one King than five hundred Kings, it is often taken, even by those who agree with it, as the usual Tory taunt at the formless tyranny of a mob. Certainly Charles, or any Tory of the period, might quite probably have uttered a taunt against the tyranny of the mob. But, in fact, in this case he meant much more exactly what he said, and what he said was perfectly correct. The Parliament was not the people, not even in the rather mechanical and clumsy way in which it is now supposed to be the people. It was based on a narrow suffrage, was honey-combed with nepotism, and mostly nominated by nobles and squires. But the case was much stronger than that. It was, in its whole attitude and action, a privileged class; a ruling class; a thing like a house of Peers and Princes. It really was, as Charles said, a House of Five Hundred Kings. It had a special Parliamentary privilege, just as he had a special Royal prerogative; and it is true to say that the King strove with the Kings. All this comes out very clearly in Mr. Bryant's narrative of the nightmare controversy of the Popish Plot. I am not going to deal here with the Popish Plot in its other aspects, least of all in its Popish aspect. My interest for the moment is not even moral, let alone religious. It is entirely intellectual, and concerned only with an intellectual admiration, in the real sense of astonishment, for that one melancholy humorist who lived through the whole of that Bedlam and remained at least the sanest of English Kings.

IN a recent discussion on Suicide, an interesting comparison was made between what is loosely called the Latin culture and what is still more loosely, and less consistently, called the Nordic or Teutonic or Germanic, according to the foreign policy at the moment. A learned writer pointed out, very truly, that for some reason or other Nordic men are more liable to kill themselves than are the men of the Mediterranean. The men of the Mediterranean are more likely to relieve their feelings by killing somebody else. And in this, I grieve to say, they have a certain half-involuntary support in my sympathies. I admit that murder must be classed among acts distinctly improper and, indeed, morally wrong. But suicide seems to me the supreme blasphemy against God and man and beast and vegetables; the attack not upon a life, but upon life itself; the murder of the universe. But that is another question, which I do not debate here. What interests me about the criticism of the two cultures is this. The critic who was sufficiently acute to notice that Latins are less prone than Teutons to this particular sort of depression and despair, naturally cast about for a cause or an explanation. And, being a modern critic, he was at once tempted to be a materialist. There is something strange in the modern mind, by which a material cause always seems more like a real cause. In the science of the nineteenth century, the material cause was generally found in physical heredity; that is to say, in Race. But Race has been rather blown upon lately; like most of the science of the nineteenth century. The critic whom I criticize took the other alternative materialistic cause; the same that has generally been favoured by Mr. Bernard Shaw. He said that most or much of the difference was due to Climate.

Now, I believe material causes count for much less in history than is now supposed. I believe that moral causes count for much more than is now supposed. I believe that the supreme factor is not even the bodily framework, or the framework of environment, but the frame of mind. I could ask for no better case, for my own argument, than this case of the suicides of all nations. It was raised on this occasion in connexion with the sad end of two famous financiers or capitalists; but that aspect need not concern us now; except, perhaps, upon one particular point. I should have thought that if there was one person to whom the argument about Climate does not apply, it is a modern millionaire. The most Nordic millionaire has no need to live in the North. An

American plutocrat could live as easily in Florida as in Maine, or pay a permanent visit to Naples instead of to Niagara. The very fact that no amount of sunshine could make him sunny, is sufficient evidence that the dark cloud was within. This, however, is a personal and even painful matter, which is no part of my argument, and with which I had not intended to deal. The point is that the critic attributes the suicide statistics to a difference of climate; and I attribute them to a difference of culture.

And it strikes me that there is a very simple test. Compare the number of suicides when the Latin world was Pagan with the number of suicides after it became Christian. The same sun shone on Brutus falling on his sword; the same blue sea smiled on Cato stabbing himself to avoid capture; the same glittering landscape of the olive and the vine was the background to the ten thousand tragedies of self-inflicted death that end the stories of the heroes of Pagan antiquity. There is no doubt that the life of those flowery lands always led to a more florid external gaiety and grace. Cleopatra blazed with blossoms and gems, and smiles, but that did not prevent her from finding an asp among the flowers. But the same fact is obvious about people considerably more respectable than Cleopatra. Those who have seen any adequate reproduction of *Julius Cæsar* will have been reminded of that sublime but alien atmosphere of the Stoic and the Republican which the imagination of Shakspere, though captive in the courtly world of the Tudors, could manage to reconstruct from the ruins of Plutarch. These Pagans of the old Latin world committed suicide not because they were prone to it as a vice, but because they were proud of it as a virtue. To explain their view of it, it would be necessary to analyse the whole tendency of their heathen mythology and philosophy. They killed themselves partly because they had too much, as the modern world has too little, of the notion of personal dignity. They killed themselves partly because they had a vaguer or more negative notion about the future life. They killed themselves because of a sort of hard despair that lies in the heart even of the heroism of the Stoic. But, anyhow, they did not kill themselves because the sun was shining or the grapes growing in clusters on the vine. Whatever is the cause of the change, it is not to be found in the climate which has not changed.

No; the test of the contrast between modern Latins and modern Teutons is exactly like the test of the contrast between modern Latins and ancient Latins. It is to be found in a frame of mind. Ever since Christianity came into the world, the Latins have been in a fighting frame of mind. Indeed, they have been, and still are, engaged in a fight; a fight about whether Christianity shall continue or no; a fight that has its ups and downs, as in the Vatican City or the secularization of Spain. But there is something in the atmosphere of the affirmation itself, even for those who prefer the denial, which has made everybody too keen on killing the enemy to retire to their tents and kill themselves. In the whole Mediterranean civilization there is a *positive* spirit. Men are either confident that they can be content with this world, or else confident that they can be convinced about the other world. Both these certainties result in relative cheerfulness and a resolve to hang on for the duration of the war. Now, in the Germanies, and generally in the northern Continental countries, the whole mental atmosphere is different. It is an atmosphere of introspective melancholy and a sort of spiritual sulks. It is exactly described in a phrase used by Mr. Augustine Birrell about Hazlitt: in the midst of the mind a black pool of metaphysics. It is a world in which men are not so much fighting religion as wandering away from it, into wildernesses of subjective speculation. It is full of scepticism, but it is not without sentimentalism; and the combination produces pessimism. It is not surprising that the pessimism sometimes produces suicide. It is the world of isolated sages, not of anti-clerical mobs or clerical congregations. From the North come the Nietzsches and the Schopenhauers, and all who, in defiance of the old name of natural philosophy, insist on inventing an unnatural philosophy. That unnatural philosophy is a third thing, quite different from natural Paganism or supernatural Christianity. It is a mood, a somewhat morbid mood, but it is the result of certain ideas in the mind; and an Eskimo does not become a suicidal maniac because he lives in the north, nor a negro a Provençal troubadour because he has a place in the sun.

THERE is a section, perhaps a small section, of Modern Youth which certainly strikes its elders as hard and sceptical and selfish. And of these it is customary to say that they are Pagans. It suddenly flashed across me yesterday (as one of those obvious truths that evade us even when they are obvious) that of course what is really the matter with them is that they have lost their Paganism.

I do not say, as so many journalists say, that they have lost their Christianity. For it is the quite simple and sober truth that most of them never had any. It is not their fault, though every day that passes convinces me more and more that it is their misfortune. But the notion, so common in novels and newspapers, that this new generation has rebelled against old-fashioned orthodoxy is sheer stark historical ignorance. It is the worst of all kinds of historical ignorance; ignorance of the historical events we have seen ourselves. It is absurd to say that a young man of nineteen who mixes cocktails and Communism in a studio rag in Chelsea is rebelling against Victorian Virtue or the Family Bible. You might

as well say that a young buck of the Regency who
wrenched off door-knockers and fought with watchmen
was rebelling against the Puritans of 1649 or the tyranny
of Oliver Cromwell. You might as well say that the
Cavaliers who revelled at The Cock in the reign of
Charles II were rising in just revolt against the usurpa-
tion of Richard III. No very laborious historical learning
will be needed to perceive that there is something wrong
in the calculation somewhere, if only because it skips
about four or five generations that come in between. So
does the cant explanation about Youth breaking away
from grim old religious dogmas skip several generations
in between. The boys and girls who are painting the
town piebald today are not the children of the old Puritan bankers with their Family Prayers or the old Protestant parsons with their Family Bibles. They are the
children of fathers and mothers who themselves grew
up on Bernard Shaw and felt like infants in the presence
of Thomas Hardy. The Young today are themselves the
children of a whole generation of sceptics and agnostics;
fathers and mothers themselves still relatively young,
and themselves brought up to all such talk. All the talk
about free thought and free love; all about Tess and
Truth; all about Candida and Candour. Even the grand-
fathers and grandmothers of the children now just beginning to play the goat were mostly of a generation

that conceived itself as liberal and progressive; like the old Radical who argues with Tanner in *Man and Superman*. Even his generation thought itself advanced; Tanner and the next generation thought itself more advanced. And we are dealing now with the children of Tanner; perhaps with the grandchildren of Tanner.

Of course, these young people do not know anything about historical Christianity; they are rather limited sort of people in a good many ways. They have heard only the latest jargon of their own generation; the last heresy that has rebelled against the last heresy but one. They are so innocent that some of them, especially the more intelligent, are actually beginning to get into touch with orthodoxy without even knowing it is orthodox. It can be seen in many casual journalistic allusions to the study of Thomism in Oxford or Paris. But it remains true that there is the other section; by no means the most intelligent, but certainly the most impudent. And of these it is true to say, as I have already said, that the whole story has moved a stage forward; or perhaps a stage back. There is no question at all of their losing Christianity. There is no question at present of their finding Christianity. But the reason why they all look as miserable as monkeys (and they do) is in this tragic and deplorable disaster: that they have all lost their Paganism.

Paganism may be compared to that diffused light that

glows in a landscape when the sun is behind a cloud. So when the true centre of worship is for some reason invisible or vague, there has always remained for healthy humanity a sort of glow of gratitude or wonder or mystical fear, if it were only reflected from ordinary objects or natural forces or fundamental human traditions. It was the glory of the great Pagans, in the great days of Paganism, that natural things had a sort of projected halo of the supernatural. And he who poured wine upon the altar, or scattered dust upon the grave, never doubted that he dealt in some way with something divine; however vague or fanciful or even sceptical he might be about the names and natures of the divinities. Wine was more than wine; it was a god. Corn was more than corn; it was a goddess. There is much doubt and dispute about how literally they understood these statements; but they certainly understood the first half of the sentence as meaning exactly what it said. They were not satisfied with realism, because they never quite lost the sense of something more real than realism. They were not content to call a spade a spade, because it was almost always a sacred spade; not only when it dug the graves of the dead, but even when it dug the garden to grow fruit for the living. They were not content with the dead certainty that eggs are eggs, because they were full of divine uncertainty about the birds, which were their signals and auguries. And this natural magic in things, mixed and modified with things greater and things less, has descended through the civilized centuries to men of every sort; not only to the mass of men who are traditionalists, but generally also to the few men who are revolutionists. Men like Shelley or Heine might get rid of religion, but they would not get rid of this great glamour of natural things, which seemed to make them preternatural. That legend still lingers from Shelley to Swinburne, from Heine to Wilde, and after that something begins to go wrong with it. It is what has gone wrong with a whole section of the rising generation.

They are not the first generation of rebels to be Pagans. They are the first generation of rebels *not* to be Pagans. The young fool, the flower of all our cultural evolution, the heir of all the ages, and the precious trust we have to pass on to posterity—the young fool can no longer be trusted to be a Pantheist, let alone a good hearty Pagan. He does not realize in the least that Bacchus has mixed his cocktail, and Pomona dropped the cherry into it. He is under the strange delusion that eggs are eggs and that spades are only spades. He entertains a perfectly extraordinary idea that wine is wine and that women are just women. He is cut off from all the secret secondary meanings and messages of things; the truths that come to the sensitive in silence; the atmosphere around every object, that is almost visible like a halo. He has lost the traditions of humanity, and rather especially the traditions of heathenry. I suppose it would not do to send out missionaries to convert him to Paganism. But he is a much more stupid and stunted and limited person since he left off being a Pagan.

SOMEBODY once said that brevity is the soul of wit, when he obviously meant to say that wit is the soul of brevity. It is obvious that the brevity is only the body, and the wit the spirit. And mere brevity, as in the statement "Cats eat rats," when left to itself, seems still to await some awakening visit of the divine fire. The proverb, however, like many other widely quoted maxims, is really as true as is consistent with meaning nearly the opposite of what it says. Economy of every kind has a great deal to do with effect of every kind. And it has often been more to the advantage of a man to say one good thing in one sentence than to say twenty good things in two thousand sentences. For the rest, the general statement of the principles of brevity would itself be brief. There would certainly be no need to discuss at length the rather obvious disadvantages of being lengthy. Most people would agree that even good writers can write too much, and that bad writers cannot write too little. Nevertheless, a particular problem has arisen in our own epoch, apart from the obvious practical complications that may arise in any epoch. Those

who earn their living by writing, as I do, always write
too much; on the other hand, there are writers at once
more leisured and more laborious who write the same
poem a hundred times, or even bring out three or four
entirely different editions of the same book. Mr. George
Moore has been an example of this paradox, and such
writers may not unfairly be said to write at once too
little and too much. But the practical problem I mean is
more recent than the realism of Mr. George Moore.
It is the question whether we more unduly increase the
mass of literature by making it difficult to stop, or by
making it easy to stop—and to begin again.

The mere forms of the older literature committed a
man to carry on for a considerable time, like a man en-
listing for the duration of the war. The modest youth
who proposed to write an epic in twelve books may have
felt epical, but hardly epigrammatical. The simple poet
who produced a tragedy in five acts could not at the last
moment turn the five-act tragedy into a three-act farce.
But now that poetry, and literature in general, is free
to appear in any form, it may naturally run to any
length or stop at any point. This may lead to brevity in
the poem, but it does not necessarily lead to brevity in
the poet. Two hundred years ago, let us say, an English
poet would sit down with the laudable intention of writing a long didactic poem on the correct cultivation of

onions, or the most advisable construction of pig-sties; all set forth in beautiful rhymed decasyllabics, brightened by entirely original selections from the Georgics and decorated by many fine flights of mythological fancy, about Ceres spreading her maternal mantle over the first onion, or Circe standing amid her pig-sties of ivory and gold. Everybody knows that the very latest poetical style has gone to the other extreme, and is not only brief, but abrupt. It is sometimes almost tactless in its introduction of the onion into the drawing-room, or the pig into the parlour. The modern poet goes straight to the point, in some short and simple lyric that runs—

> The hair of a hundred women chokes me
> With a gluttonous smell of garlic . . .

and there you are; a simple human emotion described in two spontaneous lines. Or he will write of the pig question—

> The world wobbles sickeningly,
> Like the old grey sow in the greasy morning light.

And if brevity is really the soul of wit, this must be much wittier than the long eighteenth-century poem with its classical analogies. But, considering the problem in a practical way, I should hesitate about whether

the new method will be really more brief than the old.
Supposing that it is our simple, manly, and public-
spirited purpose to stop both the poets from producing
such a vast amount of poetry, I have a notion that, in the
long run, the new poet will outstrip even the old poet
in giving the world whole libraries of poetry to burn.
After all, when the eighteenth-century poet was producing his interminable Georgic about pigs or onions,
it kept him busy; but it also kept him quiet. Quite a
long and restful period would elapse before it would even
be finished, let alone printed; there would be plenty of
time for his friends to rest and recuperate and get up
their strength to read it, or their moral strength to pretend to have read it. He did not rush about in the interval hurling isolated onions in the faces of individual
strangers. He did not bring the great grey sow with
him into society, like a lap-dog, or let loose wild herds
of Gadarene swine in the public streets. But the modern
poet's assaults on his inoffensive fellow-creatures, being
more brief and disjointed, can also be more numerous
and continuous. If he is so much intoxicated by an onion,
he may be similarly maddened by a turnip; and if pigs
for him so easily take to themselves wings and fly, the
sky they populate may soon be raining cats and dogs. I
mean that this modern habit of taking a detached image,
with or without the elucidation of its indwelling idea,

is to supersede the old reasoned arrangement of themes and thoughts. There is nothing to be said against it, except that there seems to be no end to it. And the epic of the mythological origin of onions did at least, somehow and somewhere, come at last to an end.

Granted that the old formal folios of epic and tragedy were too formal, it sometimes looks nowadays as if there would be no books except note-books or sketch-books. The notes may be short, but the note-book may be fairly long. The sketches may be smaller, but the sketch-book may be larger. Above all, the very smallness of the sketches establishes a standard which makes them more facile and therefore more frequent. I was looking the other day through a large anthology, or collection, of the most modern and advanced American poems. Most of them consisted of short impressions, with one or two arbitrary details in irregular verse; and that was all. I do not mean that they were worthless; a thousand things of the sort are worth seeing and may be worth saying. A brown trickle from a gutter makes a pool in the street, reflecting half a window and a scrap of sky; a black cluster of lamp-posts and top-hats is relieved against a strip of cold green sunset; the passing lights of a tram paint one side of a grey horse in a field a golden colour; a splash of green slime on a wall looks like sprawling fingers; and so on. Now, whether it sound egotistical or no, it is a fact that if I began to write little paragraphs in free verse on such things, I should never stop writing them. I should write thousands and thousands of them. I do not deny the truth of such sights; I am always seeing them. I do not deny the suggestiveness of such sights; I am often moved by them. I only say that if the mere recording of them constitutes poetry, there ought to be a vast amount more poetry and a great many more poets. But whether that prospect be a glorious or an alarming one, I will not venture, on my own isolated example, to decide.

WE all know that Mr. Smiles dedicated the modern world to Self-Help. Since then it has dedicated itself to Self-Hindrance, of the strangest sort, amounting often to self-strangling or self-hanging; the individualistic theory of liberty having truly given it rope enough to hang itself. It is amazing to note in how many matters the modern world started out to do one thing and has done exactly the opposite. The ethics of the economist, in the early nineteenth century, enormously exaggerated the sanctity and pride of private property. This led to a race for wealth which has not only led recently to a relapse into poverty, but to a change by which, even for the few who had more property, the property was much less private. In the nineteenth century the Northern Farmer was described as hearing the comfortable sound of "property, property, property" in the very canter of his horse's legs. Nowadays the Northern Farmer probably travels in a motor and ploughs by machinery; I know not whether strange noises from the bowels of his iron monster seem to resemble the words "mortgage" or "bankruptcy," but I am pretty certain that they do not now soothe him with the dulcet dactyls of the cantering hooves. In plain fact the Northern Farmer has much less property than he had when he started out to look for it in the presence of Mr. Alfred Tennyson. And even the property he has is much less private property, being sunk in vast semi-public undertakings or international combines, over which he certainly has no control, as he had control over his horses. The same industrial individualism which set out with no thought except private property has produced a new world in which private property is hardly ever thought of, or at least not primarily as private.

I was looking at a recent collection which contains the opinions of many famous free-thinkers about Jesus Christ. It is amusing to note how all of them differ among themselves; how one of them contradicts another and the last is always repudiated by the next. And I was specially amused to note that the earlier sceptics, like Strauss, blamed Jesus of Nazareth for his contempt for commerce and capital (then the gods of the hour), while the later sceptics, like Shaw and Wells, praised the same Jesus of Nazareth for the same contempt for the same commerce, because in the interval the sceptic had turned from an earnest Individualist to an earnest Socialist. Anyhow, it was not Christ or the Christian idea that had changed; it was only all the criticisms of all their critics. And the later sceptic actually became more orthodox than the earlier sceptic, simply by going Bolshevist. This is merely an example, for the moment, of how the whole tone of the world has changed about property in relation to privacy. The modern capitalist is more of a communist than was the old revolutionist. The real Radicals had a horror of centralization, and one of the most popular and prominent of the demagogues described a Communist as a man who "always was willing to give you his penny and pocket your shilling." The moral of this vast overturn and disappointment is obvious enough: that when private property only means private enterprise, and private enterprise only means profiteering, it will soon cease even to produce profits, and become in every sense unprofitable.

The way the world has changed about private property is proved by the fact that it is regarded as a private fad. Mr. Belloc and I, when we said first that we really did believe that private property should be private, were mildly chaffed; as if we were seeking solitude like hermits, or hoarding halfpence like misers. But I am not concerned with our particular thesis here, or with any such personal matters; I only mention this one as the most obvious of many examples of the modern world rushing one way and rebounding the other. Another example is the tangle of education. In one sense, this is supremely the educational age. In another sense, it is supremely and specially the anti-educational age. It is the age in which the Government's right to teach everybody's children is for the first time established. It is also the age in which the father's right to teach his own children is for the first time denied. It is the time in which experimentalists earnestly desire to teach a jolly little guttersnipe everything; even Criminology and Cosmic Poise and the Maya system of decorative rhythm. But it is also the time in which earnest philosophers are really doubting whether it is right to teach anybody anything; even how to avoid taking poison or falling off precipices.

But the practical difficulty of our present education is even worse. It is attempting to conduct a process, and yet it has produced a world which incessantly interrupts and reverses that process. Education is initiation; it is in its nature a progression from one thing to another; the arrangement of ideas in a certain order. A child learns to walk before he learns to skip; he learns his own alphabet before he learns the Greek alphabet. Or, if any educationist now reverses this process, he must at least have a reason for reversing it, and must therefore refuse to reverse the reversal. But the real life of our time reverses everything and has no reason for anything. The real world, that roars round the poor little gutter-boy as he goes to school, is an utterly anti-educational world. If the school is really giving any education, the world is certainly engaged day and night in ruining his education. For the world gives him things anyhow, in any order, with any result; the world gives him things without knowing that he gets them; the world gives him things meant for somebody else; the world throws things at him from morning till night, quite blindly, madly, and without meaning or aim; and this process, whatever else it is, is the exact opposite of the process of education. The gutter-boy spends about three-quarters of his time in getting uneducated. He is educated by the modern State School. He is uneducated by the modern State.

Because, as I have already ventured very delicately to hint, the modern State is in a devil of a state. It is itself the chaos and contradiction produced by that very unbalanced race after private profit that has produced its own opposite in a sort of communal confusion. Educationists have the task of putting the school in order before anybody has put the State in order. It is arguable that we ought to put the State in order before there can really be such a thing as a State School. But I will not discuss my own remedies here, which would involve indecent allusions to a third thing called the Family; now never mentioned in respectable circles. Only I think there is something wrong with a system that thus throttles itself and cuts its own throat; a world in which we cannot even paint the town red without turning it green, or set the Thames on fire without freezing it.

ROMANTICISM is usually criticized as if it were a very
ancient thing; whereas it is really a very recent thing,
and especially a very revolutionary thing. It was the
very latest Revolt of the Young, previous to the Revolt
of the Young which now attacks it. Of course, there is
a difference between Romanticism and Romance. Romance, in its healthiest sense, is as old as the world; and
even in a more special sense it is inspired by that particular intensity of colouring and pointed energy of outline which belonged to the shields, the windows, and
the pennons of mediævalism. Mediæval romance, which
was a sort of pattern for modern romance, came from
the vividness of visionary or spiritual experience leaving
a sort of glamour or glory around all experience. But it
did throw that coloured light especially on the experience of love, and, in some sense, modelled romance on
religion; as Chaucer called the legendary lovers The
Saints of Cupid. In that sense we may say that romance
belonged to the Middle Ages; and in a deeper sense
that it belonged to any ages. Romanticism, however, was
a particular modern movement, and it was in most ways

particularly modern.

It was akin to Feminism, in what is now called "putting Woman upon a pedestal." It was also akin to ideal democracy, which might well be called "putting Man upon a pedestal." Indeed, there is a curious and illuminating historical parallel between these two ideas, that seemed both new and true in the nineteenth century. I am far from saying they are not true merely because they are no longer new. I have a great deal of sympathy with both of them. I am merely noting the historical fact that, if they are not new, they were very recently regarded as new. The Republican who wore the Red Cap talked, if not as if there had never been any Republicans in the past, at least as if there were going to be nothing else except Republicans in the future. The Romantic who wore the Red Waistcoat talked as if the old world had been imprisoned in Classicism and the new world would be thrown open only to Romanticism. Each believed himself to be an extremist; but each was, in fact, a moderate who had only reached the middle of his own road, and had no real idea to what extreme it would lead. Each was a bridge hung between two ages. Each was bringing with him a living thing out of the old world, which could only perish in the new.

For one very simple thing was true both of Love and Liberty: the gods of the Romantics and the Republicans.

-C. 199 ·}-

They were both simply fragments of Christian mysticism, and even of Christian theology, torn out of their proper place, flung loosely about and finally hurled forward into an age of hard materialism which instantly destroyed them. They were not really rational ideas, still less rationalistic ideas. At least, they were never rational ideas after they had left off being religious ideas. One of them was a hazy human exaggeration of the sacramental idea of marriage. The other was a hazy human exaggeration of the brotherhood of men in God. When the Romantic laid his hand on his Red Waistcoat, and swore to George Sand or some other lady that their souls were two affinities wedded before the world was made, he was drawing on the Christian capital of the old ideas of immortality and sanctity. When he explained to his mistress in his garret the delicacy and dignity of cutting her throat and his own, and called it "the world well lost for love," he was really appealing to the old tradition of the martyr and the ascetic, who lost the world to save his soul. He was not, in any very exact sense of the word, talking sense. He was not uttering purely rational remarks; certainly not remarks that our more rationalistic generation would call rational. Often, when he had done himself particularly well with champagne and old brandy, he would let the cat out of the bag rather badly by calling the *blanchisseuse* or the artist's model "his bride in the sight of God."

Anyhow, he could not make the sort of appeals to deific faith or demoniac jealousy, which constituted the vigorous love poetry of the age of Hugo and Alfred de Musset, without implying an immortal significance in passion, which the modern realists refuse to see in mere appetite. He could not so praise love without also praising loyalty. He might not admit that there was a sacred bond between Guinevere and Arthur; but he could not write at all without assuming that there was a sacred bond between Guinevere and Lancelot. The later sex writers would refuse to admit that there is any sacred bond between anybody and anybody else. The truth is that this mystical feeling about the love of man and woman was treated so clumsily that it fell between two stools. When it was really mediæval, it could be preserved for ever in a story like that of Dante and Beatrice. When it was really modern, it simply fell to pieces, into little decaying scraps rather like wriggling worms, the hundred little loves and lusts of the modern sex novel. But the Romantics of the nineteenth century held it up in a sort of indeterminate pre-eminence; a dizzy and toppling idolatry; trying to make it at once as sacred as they thought good and as free as they found convenient. They wanted to eat their wedding-cake and have it. They wanted to make their wild wedding sacred without making it secure. They did put woman upon a pedestal; but they did not look to see if it was a solid pedestal.

Now, oddly enough, it was the same with Liberty as with Love. It was the same with the democratic ideal of political freedom for all. And Democracy is being criticized just now for exactly the same reason that Romance is being criticized just now. It is that all the sense there ever was in either of them rested on a religious idea. The nineteenth century took away the religious idea and left a sense that rapidly turned into nonsense. All men are equal because God loves all equally; and nothing can compare with that equality. But in what other way are men equal? The vague Liberals of the nineteenth century cut away the divine ground from under Democracy, and Democracy was left to stand by itself. In other words, it is left to fall by itself. Jefferson said that men were given equal rights by their Creator. Ingersoll said they had no Creator, but had received equal rights from nowhere. Even in the democratic atmosphere of America, it began to dawn on a great many people that it is very difficult to prove that men ever received the equal rights at all. In short, the Republican theory will turn out to be another form of Romance; and will be classed with the illusion of the too idealistic lover, unless it can be reconnected with the positive be-

liefs from which it was originally borrowed. The Red
Cap will follow the Red Waistcoat into the old clothes'
shop, unless it can be made something more than a
fashion, or dipped in that enduring dye that coloured
the red roses of St. Dorothy or the red cross of St.
George.

Mr. Philip Carr recently published a picturesque and
interesting sketch of the French Romantics in the great
period of Romanticism. It appeared at an appropriate
time—at about the time when we could fairly say that
artistic Paris, in that sense, had at last ceased to be gossip and had begun to be history. The admirable "Beach-
comber," in the *Daily Express,* has often made fun of
the fussy and confused "reminiscences" of men who
claim to have lived the Bohemian life of the French capital; exulting in an orgy of anarchy and anachronism;
and describing how he drank absinthe with Zola and
Chateaubriand or shared a garret with Gauguin and
Montalembert. But time sets a limit even to anachronism; it would hardly do for the most venerable journalist,
writing "Ninety-eight Years in Fleet Street" to claim to
have met Milton as well as Keats; and even Mr. Frank
Harris did not profess to have been the intimate friend
of Swift as well as Carlyle. We are now far enough away
from the French Romantics of the nineteenth century tc
judge them as we should the Pléiade in the sixteenth

century. In both cases, of course, a good many English people will entirely misjudge them and absurdly underrate them; many through a cultural, educational or acquired characteristic: a complete ignorance of French; many others by a profound, primitive, natural gift: a complete ignorance of poetry. It would be very easy to make English jokes about the French Romantics; the sort of jokes that might be made about them in *Punch*. There is even some excuse for a superficial reader, accustomed to such superficial satire, if he gains such a general impression. I mean the impression that the great geniuses of nineteenth-century Paris were all marked by three characteristics: that they all went about in crowds, frequently riotous crowds; that they each of them complained in verse that they were dwelling in a desert of unbearable loneliness; and that each of them had to be (or professed to be), for however short a period, in love with George Sand. But the weakness of all such superior Victorian patronage is that the Romantic often lived a life that was more real, not to say realistic, in its tests and risks and even privations, than the life of the patronizing Victorian. The Victorian humorist would not have liked to starve in a garret because he was a Republican or a Royalist; he would not have liked to face a Paris mob even, when it was out to kill, for a fine point of literary criticism; he certainly would not have liked

to be challenged to a duel by all the dreamy, ineffective
æsthetes in Paris; and even having a love affair with
George Sand, though to some not much more alluring
than having a heart-to-heart talk with the rhinoceros at
the Zoo, was certainly almost as dangerous. In truth it
was the jolly humorous Victorian, of the type of
Thackeray or Trollope, who was the Romantic. It was
he who lived in a world of his own; in a happy land
that was a happy dreamland; in that prosperous and
peaceful England that was a day-dream and had its day.
The French Romantics made fools of themselves in all
sorts of ways, as very clever men always do. But they
were much nearer to the taste of certain terrible things:
death and desperate faith and the fury of the poor and
abstract certitudes and even despair. They were dramatic, and even melodramatic, in their gestures; but,
after all, they were not on a stage. They lived through
real revolutions, and not unreal reforms; they lived
within striking distance of the duellist's pistol and the
rioter's pike. They followed women or visions perhaps
not worth dying for; but some of them might really
have died. Because their cries were sometimes childish,
people forget that the burnt child dreads the fire only
when it is a real fire; and the Victorian nursery always
had an efficient fireguard.

The true intellectual interest of Romanticism, now

that it has been so completely replaced by Realism, is that everybody has completely forgotten how a very recent rebellion of the young produced the first quite as much as the second. It is amusing to find the young writers of today looking back disdainfully on what they consider old-fashioned "sentiment" or "sentimentalism" or "sensibility" or "putting woman on a pedestal" or "romantic illusions about love"—all apparently under the impression that these are very venerable moral traditions of mankind that no man has ever dared to disturb till now. The truth is that all this sentiment is still a new thing; and only yesterday was *the* new thing. The romance of drooping love-locks or flowing ringlets, the fainting and the feminine sensibility, the pressed flowers and the pink albums, the Books of Beauty and the Gems of Loveliness—only yesterday, all these things were not only Youth but the Revolt of Youth. Only yesterday all these things were not only the fashion; they were even the rebellion against fashion; in the sense of the rebellion against convention. Only yesterday all these were the freaks of that Freedom by which the rising generation shocked its elders. Only yesterday all these things were Tomorrow.

Anyone who will consider the facts will see that this is no exaggeration. The albums and the keepsakes were

inscribed with endless quotations from Byron; because
Byron had been a revolutionist. We cannot now realize
the wild novelty, nay, crudity, of the young lady who
insisted on copying out Byron, instead of copying out
Cowper. We cannot feel the fact that she was gate-
crashing; that she was going the pace; that she was running around with a pretty hot crowd; but it was the
fact. And the moral of it is that nothing grows old so
quickly as what is new. The real comment upon the
simpering smile of the lady with the ringlets, as revealed
reclining with mandolin and bulbul, in the Book of
Beauty, is to send her portrait to the most modern of all
modern girls, engaged in detaching her mouth from her
face by the latest optical illusion of lip-stick, with the
old inscription: "Get you to my lady's chamber; and
tell her, let her paint an inch thick, to this favour she
must come."

More ironic than the grinning skull, more dissolvent
than dust and ashes, slower and more certain in its venge-
ance than mere death, this destiny has decreed that
The Young of every generation shall not die, but shall
live on as specimens of The Old; and especially as types
of the old-fashioned. Each generation of rebels in turn
is remembered by the next, not as the pioneers who
began the march, or started to break away from the old

conventions; but as the old convention from which only the very latest rebels have dared to break away. The moral seems to be that there may be a reward for rebels in heaven, if the Bright Young Things are looking in that direction; but there is precious little reward on earth.

THE challenge of Chaucer is that he is our one mediæval
poet, for most moderns; and he flatly contradicts all that
they mean by mediæval. Aged and crabbed historians
tell them that mediævalism was only filth, fear, gloom,
self-torture and torture of others. Even mediævalist
æsthetes tell them it was chiefly mystery, solemnity and
care for the supernatural to the exclusion of the natural.
Now Chaucer is obviously *less* like this than the poets
after the Renaissance and the Reformation. He is obviously more sane even than Shakspere, more liberal
than Milton; more tolerant than Pope; more humorous
than Wordsworth; more social and at ease with men
than Byron or even Shelley. Nay, some have doubted
whether he is not still more humane than the very latest
humanists; whether his geniality does not exceed the
rosy optimism of Aldous Huxley or the ever-bubbling
high spirits of T. S. Eliot.

Chaucer was, above all, an artist; and he was one of
that fairly large and very happy band of artists who
are not troubled with the artistic temperament. Perhaps
there was never a less typical poet, as a poet was under-

stood in the Byronic tradition of dark passions and tempestuous raiment. But, indeed, that Byronic generalization was largely founded upon Byron, or rather, on a blunder about Byron. It would be much truer to say that practically every type of human being has been also a poet, and that Byron was a Regency Buck plus poetry. Similarly, Goethe was a German professor plus poetry, and Browning was a rather commercial-looking bourgeois plus poetry, and Heine was a cynical Jew plus poetry, and Scott was a rather acquisitive gentleman farmer plus poetry, and Villon was a pickpocket plus poetry, and Wordsworth was a noodle plus poetry, and Walt Whitman was an American loafer plus poetry—for, in the art of loafing, Weary Willie could never have stood up against Unweary Walt. I have not yet heard of an American dentist or a shop-walker in a large draper's who is a poet, and I have no doubt that both of these deficiencies will soon be supplied. Anyhow, the general rule is that almost any trade or type of man can be an artist—yes, even an æsthete.

But once or twice there appears in history the artist who is the extreme antithesis of the æsthete. An artist of this kind was Geoffrey Chaucer. He was a man who always made himself useful, and not only ornamental. People trusted him, not only in the moral, but in the more purely practical sense. He was not the sort of poet

who would forget to post a letter, or post an unstamped
ode to the cuckoo instead, had the penny postage existed
in his day. He was not only given many responsible
posts, but responsible posts of many kinds. At one time
he was sent to negotiate the delicate finances of ransom
and peace with a great prince. At another time he was
sent to oversee the builders and workmen in the construction of a great public building. It has been conjec-
tured that he had some technical knowledge of architecture, and I think the descriptions of various pagan
temples and royal palaces in his poems support the con-
jecture. It is certain that he knew a good deal about the
official precedence and etiquette of the Chamberlain's
Office; he was a witness upon a point of heraldry in an
important trial. Though his relations to the Court, during and after the *débâcle* of Richard II, are covered with
some obscurity, it is certain that, for the greater part of
his life at least, he performed job after job, of the most
quaintly different kinds, to the increasing satisfaction of
his employers. He was emphatically, as the vulgar
phrase goes, a man of the world.

But through all these tasks the lyric element flowed
out of him quite naturally, as a man will whistle or sing
while he is potting a shrub or adding up a column of
figures. He never seemed to have felt any particular
strain or dislocation between the world in which he was

a man of the world and that other world of which he was one of the immortals. He had that sort of temper in which there is no antithesis of Sense and Sensibility. He does not seem to have quarrelled with many people, even in that very quarrelsome transition time; and he does not seem to have quarrelled with himself. Being a Christian, he was ready to accuse himself when he was seriously considering the question; but that is something quite different from the sort of constant unconscious friction between different parts of the mind which has marred the happiness of so many artists and poets.

I do not mean merely that the poetry of Chaucer, like the poetry of Dante, was in the higher sense a harmony. I mean that it was in the ordinary human sense a melody. It remained not only unspoilt, but unmixed; uncomplicated by the complexities of living, whether they were actually there or no. It is unfortunate that the word "mood" is almost always used of a sombre or secretive mood; and that we do not convey the idea that a man was in merry mood when we say merely that he was moody. For there was truly a special thing that may be called the Chaucerian mood, and it was essentially merry. There are any number of passages of pathos, and one or two passages of tragedy, but they never make us feel that the mood has really altered, and it seems as if the man speaking is always smiling as he speaks. In other words, the thing which is supremely Chaucerian is the Chaucerian atmosphere, an atmosphere which penetrates through all particular persons and problems; a sort of diffused light which lies on everything, whether tragic or comic, and prevents the tragedy from being hopeless or the comedy from being cruel. No art critic, however artistic, has ever succeeded in describing an atmosphere. The only way to approach it is to compare it with another atmosphere. And this Chaucerian mood is very like the mood in which (before it became merely vulgarized by cant or commercialism) some of the greatest of modern English writers have praised Christmas.

Chaucer was wide enough to be narrow; that is, he could bring a broad experience of life to the enjoyment of local or even accidental things. Now, it is the chief defect of the literature of today that it always talks as if local things could only be limiting, not to say strangling; and that anything like an accident could only be a jar. A Christmas dinner, as described by a modern minor poet, would almost certainly be a study in acute agony: the unendurable dullness of Uncle George, the cacophonous voice of Aunt Adelaide. But Chaucer, who sat down at the table with the Miller and the Pardoner, could have sat down to a Christmas dinner with the heaviest uncle or the shrillest aunt. He might have been amused at them, but he would never have been angered by them, and certainly he would never have insulted them in irritable little poems. And the reason was partly spiritual and partly practical; spiritual because he had, whatever his faults, a scheme of spiritual values in their right order, and knew that Christmas was more important than Uncle George's anecdotes; and practical because he had seen the great world of human beings, and knew that wherever a man wanders among men, in Flanders or France or Italy, he will find that the world largely consists of Uncle Georges. This imaginative patience is the thing that men want most in the modern Christmas, and if they wish to learn it I recommend them to read Chaucer.

I saw in an illustrated paper—which sparkles with
scientific news—that a green-blooded fish had been
found in the sea; indeed, a creature that was completely
green, down to this uncanny ichor in its veins, and very
big and venomous at that. Somehow I could not get it
out of my head, because the caption suggested a perfect
refrain for a Ballade: A green-blooded fish has been
found in the sea. It has so wide a critical and philosophical application. I have known so many green-blooded
fish on the land, walking about the streets and sitting
in the clubs, and especially the committees. So many
green-blooded fish have written books and criticisms of
books, have taught in academies of learning and founded
schools of philosophy, that they have almost made
themselves the typical biological product of the present
stage of evolution. There is never a debate in the House
of Commons, especially about Eugenics or The Com-
pulsory Amputation of Poor People, without several
green-blooded fishes standing up on their tails to talk.
There is never a petition, or a letter to the Press, urg-
ing the transformation of taverns into teashops or local

museums, without a whole string of green-blooded fish hanging on to the tail of it, and pretty stinking fish too. But for some reason the burden of this non-existent Ballade ran continually in my head, and somehow turned my thoughts in the direction of poisonous monsters in general; of all those dragons and demi-dragons and devouring creatures which appear in primitive stories as the chief enemies of man. It has been suggested that these legends really refer to some period when prehistoric man had to contend with huge animals that have since died out. And then the thought occurred to me: Suppose the primitive heroes killed them just when they were dying out. I mean, suppose they would have died out, even if the Cave Man had sat comfortably in his Cave and not troubled to kill them.

Suppose Perseus turned the sea-monster into a rock at the very moment when it was well on its way to becoming a fossil. Suppose St. George arrived, not only just before the death of the Princess, but just before the death of the Dragon. Suppose he burst in, rather tactlessly, so to speak, on the deathbed of the dragon, and only finished him off with a lance when the dragon-doctor had done the real work with a lancet. In short, is it possible that the heroes might have saved themselves the trouble of fighting, if they had only felt the pulse or taken the temperature of the expiring foe of mankind? The dragon is always represented with wide-open jaws, darting out a forked and flaming tongue. But perhaps he is only putting his tongue out to be examined by his private physician. Perhaps all the monsters, when they appear in song and story, were in a bad way, physically as well as morally. Now I come to think of it, that might explain the green-blooded fish that was found in the sea. Perhaps he is not a species, but a disease. Perhaps the green-blooded fish was suffering, if not exactly from anæmia, at least from some subtle form of chloræmia pisciana, or whatever this obscure malady will be called when it is discovered. I suppose a fish in the sea could hardly be green with seasickness. And anyhow, there are biological theorists even on land, who have lately begun to look rather fishy.

The fancy might make many variants in the fairy-tales. They always narrate how the cavern of the monster or giant is surrounded by the bones of thousands of victims. We can imagine the hero carefully counting them and making calculations about the stage of indigestion at which any monster must have arrived after such a meal. In the special department of Giants there is a story about Jack the Giant-Killer and a hasty-pudding, which the Giant at least devoured. I do not know what a hasty-pudding is, but I gather that in this case the meal was somewhat hasty. All this could not be good for the health of Giants as a class. And Dickens, who had known several Giants, as they appear in travelling-shows, testifies to their delicate constitutions. But I admit that, while my rambling subconsciousness ran on this ancient theme, I was beginning to think of its modern application. I sometimes wonder whether it is worth while to attack every monster of modern anarchy and absurdity as it appears in the realm of thought, or whether they would kill themselves even if they were not killed. Sometimes they seem to kill themselvs almost too fast to be killed. Some I can remember making war on for months who have now been dead for years. I can remember giants of blasphemy or barbaric philosophy; giants so gigantic that they seemed not only to darken the earth, but block out the heavens. They defied the world like Goliath, and all were warned against accepting the challenge, in sight of all the bones about their caverns. But now it is their own bones that are scattered, and even a rag-and-bone man will hardly stoop to pick them up.

For instance, there was Haeckel and the hard concrete Materialism of his day. For years on end I filled my life with fighting Mr. Blatchford and others about it, and pointing out the fallacies, not to say falsehoods, of Haeckel. And where is he now? Mr. Blatchford has forgotten all about Haeckel, and so has everybody else. The new men of science have completely repudiated him. But I remember when every new man of science, and especially of the new science of sociology or eugenics (a green-blooded fish has been found in the sea), accepted him as the founder of a new religion. And when Mr. Belloc wrote the envoi of another Ballade—

> Prince, if you meet upon a bus
> A man who makes a great display
> Of Dr. Haeckel, argue thus,
> The wind has blown them all away—

it really sounded like an audacity or a daring prophecy. Whereas now it sounds like a truism, because it has come true.

Then there was Lombroso, and all the quackery that was called Criminology. I can remember when the name of Lombroso was like the name of Newton or of Faraday; but I do not often see it mentioned now, least of all among men of science. It is to the enduring glory of Mr. H. G. Wells that even in those days, though on the materialist side in many matters, he protested against the premature dogmatism of the prigs who talked about "the criminal skull" or "the criminal ear," and who called the young and earnest to stamp out hereditary criminal tendencies by selection or segregation (a green-blooded fish has been found in the sea). Was it worth while to argue against the great Science of Criminology in the later nineteenth century? The dragon would have died a natural death, if anything about him could be natural.

I could give any number of other cases; of other controversies with things I thought dominant which were in fact dying; which are in fact dead. There was the proposal that people too poor to bring actions for libel should be put on a Black List as blackguards who were too fond of beer (a green-blooded fish has been found in the sea); there was the absurd theory that being too fond of beer is hereditary, and the proposal (moved by the fish) that the beer-drinker should be forbidden children. There was the whole assumption that anything done by a State Department would be perfect and that Supervisors are Supermen. That was once our nightmare; but flogging it was flogging a dead horse, or at least a dying horse, and I rather repent of my inhumanity.

THERE used to be, and possibly is, a mysterious institution for young ladies known as a finishing-school. The chief case against it was that, in certain instances, it meant finishing an education without ever beginning it. In any case, this is what is the matter with a great many modern institutions, and with none more than those delivering judgment on the history of feminine education and generally of feminine affairs. The curse of nearly all such judgments is the journalistic curse of having heard the latest news; that is, of having heard the end of the story without having even heard of the beginning. We talk of people not knowing the A B C of a subject, but the trouble with these people is that they do know the X Y Z of a subject without knowing the the A B C.

This morning I read an article in a very serious magazine in which the writer quoted the remark of Byron that a certain sort of romantic love "is woman's whole existence." The writer then said that the first people who ever challenged this view were the revolutionary Suffragettes at the end of the nineteenth century. The truth is that the first people who ever maintained this view were the revolutionary Romantics at the beginning of the nineteenth century. The habit of giving to romantic love this extravagant and exclusive importance in human life was itself an entirely modern and revolutionary thing, and dates from the romantic movement commonly traced to Rousseau, but I think much more truly to be traced to the influence of the German sentimentalists. Most people who curse Rousseau have never read Rousseau, or have only read the *Confessions* and not the *Contrat Social*. The critics read the *Confessions*, if only to condemn them; because the critics themselves are modern romantics and sentimentalists; men who like Confessions and dislike Contracts. The critics hate or avoid the *Contrat Social*, not because it is sloppy and sentimental (for it is not), but because it is hard and clear and lucid and logical. Rousseau had his emotional weaknesses as an individual, like other individuals, but he was not an eighteenth-century philosopher for nothing. What the moderns dislike about him is not the silliness of his confessions, but the solidity of his convictions, and the fact that, like the old theologians, he could hold general ideas in a hard-and-fast fashion. When it comes to defining his fundamentals, Rousseau is as definite as Calvin. They were both ruthless theorists from Geneva, though one preached the theory of pessimism and the other the theory of optimism. I am not maintaining that I agree with either, but Rousseau would be as useful as Calvin, in teaching some of his critics how to criticize.

But Rousseau is a parenthesis. Wherever the real Romantic Movement came from, whether from the German forests or the Genevan lake, it was a recent and revolutionary business as compared with history as a whole. But it is obvious that the ordinary modern critic is entirely ignorant of history as a whole. He knows that his mother read Tennyson and his grandmother read Byron. Beyond that, he can imagine nothing whatever; he supposes that his great-great-grandmothers and their great-great-great-grandmothers had gone on reading Byron from the beginning of the world. He imagines that Byron, who was a disinherited and disreputable rebel to the last, has been an established and conventional authority from the first. He therefore supposes that all women, in all ages, would have accepted the prehistoric Byronic commandment: that the Byronic sort of romantic passion was the sole concern of their lives. Yet it is certain that women have had a great many other concerns, and have been attached to a great many other convictions. They have been priestesses, prophetesses, empresses, queens, abbesses, mothers, great housewives, great letter-writers, lunatics founding sects, bluestockings keeping salons, and all sorts of things. If you had said to Deborah the mother in Israel, or Hypatia the Platonist of Alexandria, or Catherine of Siena, or Joan of Arc, or Isabella of Spain, or Maria Theresa of Austria, or even to Hannah More or Joanna Southcott, that Byronic love was "woman's whole existence," they would all have been very indignant and most of them flown into a towering passion. They would have asked in various ways whether there was no such thing as honour, no such thing as duty, no such thing as glory, no such thing as great studies or great enterprises, no such thing as normal functions and necessary labours; incidentally, we may add, no such thing as babies. They differed a great deal in their type of vocation and even in their theory of virtue, but they all had some theory of virtue that went a little further than that. Up to a particular moment in the eighteenth century, practically every thinking person would have accepted the colossal common sense expressed by a French poet of the seventeenth century: *"L'amour est un plaisir; l'honneur est un devoir."*

Then came the extreme emphasis on romance among the Victorians; for the Victorians were not notable for their emphasis on virtue, but for their emphasis on romance. But Queen Victoria lived so long, and the Victorian Age was such an unconscionably long time dying, that by the time Mr. Bernard Shaw and others began what they called a realistic revolt against romance, the sentimental German movement seemed to be not only as old as Victoria, but as old as Boadicea. It is highly typical, for instance, that Mr. Bernard Shaw, in one of his earliest criticisms, complained of the convention according to which anybody was supposed to have "penetrated into the Holy of Holies" so long as he was content to say that "Love is Enough." But, as a matter of fact, the very phrase "Love is Enough" did not come to him from any conventional or classical authority; not even from any conventional or conservative Victorian. It came from a book by a Socialist and Revolutionist like himself; from a book recently published by William Morris, who held then the exact position that Mr. Shaw himself holds now: the position of the Grand Old Man of Socialism.

Of course, the anti-romantic movement led by Shaw, like the romantic movement led by Byron, had gone forward blindly and blundered in every sort of way. The modern world seems to have no notion of preserving different things side by side, of allowing its proper and proportionate place to each, of saving the whole varied heritage of culture. It has no notion except that of simplifying something by destroying nearly everything; whether it be Rousseau breaking up kingdoms in the name of reason, or Byron breaking up families in the name of romance, or Shaw breaking up romances in the name of frankness and the formula of Ibsen. I myself value very highly the great nineteenth-century illumination of romantic love, just as I value the great eighteenth-century ideal of right reason and human dignity, or the seventeenth-century intensity, or the sixteenth-century expansion, or the divine logic and dedicated valour of the Middle Ages. I do not see why any of these cultural conquests should be lost or despised, or why it is necessary for every fashion to wash away all that is best in every other. It may be possible that one good custom would corrupt the world, but I never could see why the second good custom should deny that the first good custom was good. As it is, those who have no notion except that of breaking away from romance are being visibly punished by breaking away from reason. Every new realistic novel serves to show that realism, when entirely emptied of romance, becomes utterly unreal. For romance was only the name given to a love of life which was something much larger than a life of love, in the Byronic sense. And anything from which it has passed is instantly corrupt and crawling with worms of death.

IT is now much discussed among the learned whether art should abolish morality by calling it convention. It might well be discussed among the wise whether art should even abolish convention. But what seems very queer to me is this: that modern art has so often abolished morality without abolishing convention. I mean that very tame and timid conventions, the remains of rather fragil and artificial styles of writing, do still manage to run side by side with complete licence or laxity about much more important things. It seems as if people could get rid of the commandments, but not of the conventions. I will give only one small example, which has struck me again and again in reading the most modern novels.

In those modern novels there are types of women, and descriptions of women, which might have brought a blush to the cheek of Petronius or been considered a little too coarse for the refinement of Rabelais. But in those descriptions there are still certain conventions, really unreal conventions, exactly as they were in the Victorian works of Miss Porter or Miss Procter. Again and again, the modern reader may read a sentence like this: "Peter had already noticed a smiling, blue-eyed girl, with a bright, shingled head, slip in among the new-comers, suspected of being gate-crashers, who thronged the door." Or the sentence may run: "Slim, lithe, and brown-eyed, with a delicate and fiery tan, Joan stood poised on the distant rock, about to dive." There are a hundred other examples; but all habitually assume that the first thing that anybody notices about a woman is the colour of her eyes. Now, it is perfectly possible to be on tolerably intimate terms with a person for a long time and yet to be quite unable to recall suddenly the colour of his or her eyes. And certainly nobody ever saw the colour of a stranger's eyes all the way across a ball-room in Mayfair, a big studio in Chelsea, or the wide sands of the Lido. One would suppose that a girl's blue eyes were enormously big blue lanterns, and shone afar off like the green and red lanterns of a railway signal. That one little sentimental trick or tradition makes hundreds of literary descriptions of human beings ring quite false, and the most lavish and generous supply of general moral barbarism and baseness cannot wholly make up the loss.

What a man sees first about a woman, or anybody else, is the type; whether it is, for instance, the type that flows in long lines, with long features, the type that an artist would draw in profile; or whether it has the face that is most itself when seen fully in front, flat against a background; especially the sort of square and open face, the face that is generally that of a fighter, and, however beautiful it may be, has always a touch of the monkey. A man can distinguish those two types from each other across the largest hall or the widest sands, almost as easily as he could distinguish a horse from a cow or a stag. He might distinguish a hundred things about the rank or the culture or even the character; he could make inferences from the poise and the walk and the gesture. He could do it all at a distance, at which it would be as impossible to see blue eyes in the girl's head as to see blue stones in the girl's engagement ring. Yet I have seen that little artificiality of description a hundred times in a day's reading, in turning over the tales even of able and ambitious modern novelists. It is a small matter; indeed, it is the point that it is a small matter; it is too small to be seen, and yet it is always reported. But it happens to illustrate a curious sort of concealed convention that runs underneath much modern writing that considers itself most unconventional. In more showy things the realists remember to be shameless; but in these little things they do not remember to be realistic.

I knew a lady, with a very hearty sense of humour,

whose business it happened to be to write frankly conventional romances for the old frankly conventional Press, the Press that provided healthy but somewhat sentimental serials and novelettes. She got great fun out of her functions; and she told me once that she had written a long serial romance, with a stately and tragic heroine, only to be told at the end that the public, or at least the publishers, insisted on a *petite* and sparkling heroine. With a noble calm, disdaining to alter a single incident in the narrative, she merely went through the whole manuscript, altering black eyes to blue eyes. When she came to the line, "He gazed into Amanda's dark, unfathomable eyes," she merely crossed out the adjectives and wrote "blue and sparkling" on the top. Of course, it was not all a matter of eyes; she had to make some modification about dress and demeanour. Where she had written "Amanda swept across the lawn," the alteration of one word made it "Amanda tripped across the lawn." That, by the way, is another of the old conventions that linger even in the new unconventionality. Girls still sometimes trip in the grimmest realistic studies. Novelists still sometimes trip over that antiquated booby trap. I never saw anybody trip, except somebody who tripped over a hassock and fell on his nose, to the satiric enlivenment of the human race. Anyhow, Amanda's large and shady hat grew less large and shady, and was turned up with a rose or something; her raiment grew less sweeping and severe; but nothing else needed any alteration. And it sometimes seems to me that many who write in the most revolutionary fashion write quite as much according to a revolutionary formula. They merely go through their own story and put in the terms which are supposed to make the heroine chic or distinguished, according to the momentary modern conventions of unconventionality. The heroine has no more real individuality, amid all the fuss of individualism, than the adaptable Amanda whose eyes turned so easily from black to blue.

Perhaps what we call realistic descriptions are bound to be conventional because they are bound to be fashionable. They are bound to emphasize exactly the points which one particular period thinks important; which will be exactly the points which the next period will think unimportant. Hence we have the paradox that the noblest compliments to women have not been direct descriptions, but indirect descriptions. The direct compliment would deal with all the details that pass; the indirect compliment with the impression which does not pass. Archæologists have worked out a complete theory of the costume of Helen of Troy, which seems to have consisted of a straw sun-bonnet, a Zouave jacket, and high-heeled shoes. If Homer had written a realistic description, it would have seemed to us a rather vulgar description. The dress of the fourteenth century was more dignified, but not more natural; and if Dante had described Beatrice in the exact garb she wore it might have seemed to us at once extravagant and stiff. But ages shall pass and civilizations shall perish, and time shall never turn the keen edge of that great indirect compliment, that older and wiser fashion of describing the effect and not the external instruments. As when Dante, seeing his lady upon the height, felt only like the legendary monster whom the taste of a strange food had turned into a god. Or Homer was content to let us listen to the grumbling of the Trojans against the cause of the Trojan War, and then to that great sudden silence that fell upon them, full of light and understanding, when Helen came forth upon the wall.

THE debate about legalizing Sweepstakes dies slowly away, like the galloping echoes of the Derby; and even where it continues, it is rather typical of the time and country that it is more concerned with law than with logic. It is clear that in practice the nation has largely abandoned the Puritan sentiment that was behind some of its older laws; but it has been rather a change of sentiment than a change of statement. Few people really remember what was the actual ethical theory that gave to all betting the bad name of gambling. But fewer still, I fancy, could state their own new ethical theory in favour of betting, or distinguish it from the gambling that is really bad. Even when we were Puritans we were not really precisians. In other words, England, even when it was strict in discipline, was not really strict in doctrine. Certainly, at least, it was not really strict in definition. Consequently, I do not really know what the moral theory of the anti-betting men was; and I do not believe they knew themselves. My own morality, which is not my own, but that of the ancient moral culture of Christendom, is of course simple enough. I have a right to bet what I have a right to lose. If I choose to sit on the wild seashore and occupy my whole holiday in throwing stones into the sea, I am also entitled, if I choose, to vary the monotony by throwing into the sea the large moon-stone tie-pin which is the ornament of my neckties and the admiration of my neighbours, or to hurl into the same sea-waves the heavy cairn-gorm brooch bequeathed by my Aunt Jemima; always supposing I can do the latter without unjustly lacerating Aunt Jemima's feelings, here or in heaven. I have as much right to throw the more expensive stones into the sea as to throw the cheaper ones; so long as it is only at my own expense and not something beyond my lawful expenditure; which would probably turn out to be at somebody else's expense. So far as that goes, I am perfectly justified in throwing away my celebrated tie-pin or my aunt's brooch for the mere momentary pleasure of one sublime gesture; for the satisfaction of feeling like Polycrates or the great Doge of Venice wedding the sea. It is a mere luxury to chuck them, as it is a mere luxury to cherish them; I only keep them for a lark, and I only lose them for a lark. If a man is justified in throwing a pearl like a pebble into the sea at Margate, knowing it will not return, he is justified in throwing it on the table at Monte Carlo or putting it on a horse at Ascot: with a chance that it may return. But he is not justified, for instance, in throwing the baby into the sea, though many at Margate have felt tempted to do so. Nor is he justified in risking the baby's milk or the money for the baby's clothes at Ascot or Monte Carlo; and nobody will deny that many have done this, and that much evil has come of it. But the principle is at least clear, and presents no problem to those who hold it.

I have sometimes thought that the philosophy of betting bears some resemblance to something else, which may be called the philosophy of guessing. There is in the literary or intellectual world an operation which is somewhat similar to that of honest betting in the sporting world. It occurs especially in the case of English literature; because in England it so often happens that the author is the amateur. It often happens, also, that the amateur can give valuable hints to the professional. But those hints ought always to be given in a certain light and sporting spirit, not unlike the guesses of the better sort of gambler. The outsider ought not to give the whole weight of his word or reputation to suggestions he could not substantiate in all their details. If he does, he tends to become the crank or even the quack, the awful and appalling sort of amateur who sits down to prove to you that Mary Queen of Scots wrote Shakspere or that the name of Lord Kitchener is inscribed in the measurements of the Great Pyramid. But I have often thought there might be a place for intelligent guesswork which admits that it is guesswork. There might even be a place for a fanciful theory, if it was avowedly fanciful. I confess I have suffered many things from the sort of man who has a theory that Bacon wrote Shakspere, when he does really believe it. But I had great fun in working out a theory that Shakspere wrote Bacon, because I did not in the least believe it. In the course of turning it into a sketch, which was no more than a skit, I found myself discovering much more than I had known before of the real truth about the Elizabethan and Jacobean epoch. In the same way, many a man has really put hard cash in his pocket at Newmarket, or the Grand National from a bet that he made merely as a joke; and my contention is that he deserved his luck, so long as he really made it as a joke. In the case of history and similar sciences, it might be possible to draw up a rich and flattering analogy to the Turf. The dons of Oxford and Cambridge, the professors and professional historians, who are often, indeed, bookmakers, may be compared to bookies. The dream or fancy thrown out by the mere literary amateur may be compared to the dark horse in the very loose box of his light and irresponsible brain. But the dark horse always gives him a good run for his money. And it is justified, so long as it does not run away with the whole of his money; that is, with the whole of his serious reputation and peace of mind. I think there ought to be a special class of spirited and fanciful guesses; potshots at the possibilities of history; suggestions that should only suggest, but might be really suggestive. They would form a third type of literature, between the solemn stolidity of the academies and the solemn lunacy of the cranks.

For instance, I once had a notion of writing an essay, making a suggestion about King Arthur. Now I am not in the least qualified to maintain an entirely serious and solid thesis about King Arthur. A man would really have to be an exceptional scholar and specialist, in about five different departments, before he could deal in that fashion with King Arthur. He would have to know all about Celtic legend and literature, Welsh and Cornish and all the rest; he would have to have a thorough grasp of the decline and fall of the Roman Empire, its military maps and methods; he would have to be steeped in French chivalry and romance to separate the mediæval from the older elements; he would have to understand the real Christian and Catholic origins, and date and distinguish between the Glaston Thorn and the Grail; he would have to be a nailer at strategy and a whale at place-names. I am none of these things, and yet I had quite a nice little notion about King Arthur. It would afford a pleasant evening's amusement for a party of dons, pulling it to pieces. And, for all I know, something might come out of it; even out of its refutation. I will not describe the theory here beyond saying that it began with the curious fact, that the first three or four chroniclers who mention King Arthur do not even call him King Arthur. But I will reserve it for some dull and rainy afternoon, in some quiet isolated country house, where there are dons who want something to play with.

THE other day I was stricken by a great grief; I will not go so far as to say that I burst into tears at the breakfast table, but I believe I must have uttered a deep and hollow groan, to the surprise and alarm of my family. For I found that no less a person than the Dean of St. Paul's had used the now common phrase about people "making good." He said, in support of his recognized preference for the produce of the super-villas over that of the slums, that there is "nothing snobbish" in recognizing the superiority of "those who have made good" over the wastrels and misfits, whom he seems to conceive as constituting the whole population of the poorer quarters of the modern city. Talking about "making good" seems to me much worse than snobbish, for it is not even English. And if, as satirists have said, the English have some tendency to be snobs, they might at least be content to be English snobs. Now, this is very sad and strange; hence my outburst of emotion at the breakfast table. For, in the ordinary way, Dean Inge writes most beautiful English; sometimes really splendid English. He writes the sort of strong English that is founded on strong Latin, not the more modern sort that is in theory Nordic and in practice Yankee—or sometimes even Cockney. This again is curious, for in a way his practice is better than his precept; and it does not so much matter if he is Nordic in his theory of history, since he is entirely Mediterranean in his practice of scholarship. He is always cursing the Latin culture, and no man's culture is more entirely Latin.

But I am not dealing here with the many matters on which I differ from the Dean, or even those on which the Dean differs from himself. I will not pause here to attempt to dispel that extraordinary nightmare that appears to brood upon his brain; the general notion that all the inhabitants of West Ham or Hoxton are hunchbacks, homicidal maniacs, or hereditary cripples, every man born with one leg and one eye. I will not stop to explain that the Old Kent Road is not exclusively inhabited by wealthy men who have wasted their fortunes and become "wastrels," and that if poor men, as well as rich men, may sometimes be "misfits," it is the business of a philosopher to criticize not only them, but the framework in which they were expected to fit. But all this is an old argument, and my present concern with the Dean is not to express a difference from his opinions, but rather a tender solicitude for his style. I write not in a spirit of antagonism, but of admiration; of admiration tinged with alarm. By all means let him defend, in his own brilliant and lucid fashion, what he calls the upper middle class. Let him indulge in the most spirited, sparkling, and daring paradoxes about these ladies and gentlemen. Let him say that they do good, that they are good; but not, O not, in the name of our noble tongue and heritage, that they make good!

I know not where that man hides and cowers, probably among the millions who had fled to the criminal dens and lairs of the United States, who actually originated the phrase about "making good." If I knew who he was, I would write a life of him; having first killed him, of course, to make the biography complete. He must have been rather a great man in his own perverted and repulsive fashion, for he managed to sum up the supreme essential falsehood of a whole century and a whole civilization in one exactly appropriate phrase, a phrase that is all the more appropriate because it is idiotic. He must be rather like one of the great poisoners, for indeed he has poisoned the whole modern mind. He must be much more than one of the great conspirators, for, as Mr. Wells would say, it is an entirely open conspiracy. He has managed to put all the current contemporary philosophies into one phrase that means nothing. Everybody whose instincts are on the side of such sophistry instantly seizes on it, because of its ambiguity. With one single twist of bad grammar or bad logic, it tangles up together the two things that have been in sharp contrast and contradiction in every decent religion or moral system in history—the idea of moral greatness and the idea of mere material success. And yet making good is not even making sense. It will not really serve to make a sentence, let alone a good sentence or a true sentence.

Thus we can say of one of these abject beings who happen to live in Hoxton or the Harrow Road that he makes good beer-barrels; that he makes good drain-pipes; that he makes good penny-whistles or good pork-pies; but not that he makes good. It does not make sense; it does not make a sentence. And this ambiguous phrase about making good was invented because it was ambiguous; it was invented by the man who did not make pies or pipes or barrels or anything in the East End, but only scooped the profit on other men's work and went off with it to live in the West End. That is all that is meant by making good. It did not matter so much so long as people refrained from describing it as making good; so long as they were content to describe it as making money. Considered merely as one of the mild forms of rascality very common among human beings, it might really be described as mild or even as human. But by the fatal and blasting hypocrisy of this one American catchword, it was transformed from a matter of unmoral adventure to a matter of thoroughly immoral morality. The phrase "making good," merely because it contains the word "good," always carries some shadowy suggestion that the man who has merely done well for himself must also have really done well; done well as in the old creeds and codes of morals; done well in the sight of God and humanity. And that is not merely immorality, it is blasphemy; for it is practically saying that the selfish man is the saint, and that Judas with the bag is greater than Jesus with the cross.

Meanwhile, nothing but this fog of a phrase, like a real London fog choking the streets round St. Paul's Cathedral, could have so completely hidden the facts of the modern social situation from the Dean of St. Paul's. If making good meant making good things, pipes or barrels or what not, it would be obvious that people go on doing it, generation after generation, as much in the lower class as in his favourite upper middle class. I wonder how often these sages of the upper middle class stop to think what London would be like, if all the lower classes were really such fools as they suppose. What would London in a fog be like, for instance, if enormous numbers of cabmen and carmen, and men controlling traffic, were most of them drunken or incompetent? The fact is that the wastrels and the misfits, or in other words the working classes, are making good all the time. They are making good day and night; they are making good from minute to minute; or none of us would get to the end of an hour's journey. The Dean is quite entitled to praise the sort of clerical or academic family that he himself comes of; to note the virtues they really possess; and doubtless there are virtues which are easier for such a clergyman than for such a cabman. But it is very far from being self-evident that every clergyman is more successful with his sermon than any cabman with his service. Both the clergyman and the cabman may be good men; but the more they are really good men, the less they will be attracted by the ideal of making good.

| XXXIX | *On Making Good—II* |

A VERY eminent and distinguished critic has done me the honour to criticize, in a private letter, the remarks I made recently in disparagement of the phrase "making good." He agrees with me, or at least he disagrees with Dean Inge, in so far as to admit that the Dean's controversial use of the term was a sophistry. We should not differ very much about the social views involved. But about the verbal and grammatical matter my correspondent does not agree, and he is prepared to maintain that the phrase "making good" can be defended as a form of English idiom. He says, very truly, that it is possible to use it in a much more natural and ordinary way than it is used in the particular argument of the Dean of St. Paul's. He says that the ordinary honest plumber, of whom I spoke, might be said to have made good in carrying out a small job or contract, and that there would be nothing odd about the phrase. It is possible, of course, that the Dean would decline to accept the arbitration of the plumber, as much as I should decline to accept the arbitration of the Dean. But the point seems to me worth a word or two of further elucidation and explanation.

First, upon the primary point, I am disposed to stand firm; I mean the point of the logic of grammar. For I am, I confess, so degenerate a Latin type of mind that I think there ought to be some logic in grammar. And it seems to me a simple fact that "to make" is a transitive verb, and must have an object or accusative. We can make a plumber good, or make a Dean good, or even make a poor bewildered and overwrought journalist, writing in a weekly illustrated paper, good; but we cannot make good. If it is an allowable idiom, it must be an exception and not a rule; and it must be an exception by some exceptional process, such as that of depending upon words that are "understood." I know that this practice does exist; nor can the most logical Latin wholly condemn it, for it exists even in the logical Latin language. There is a form, which I remember learning laboriously in the Latin grammar as a boy, by which some such word as *officium*, for instance, could be understood. It is allowable to say in Latin: "It is of a good man to worship the gods," or "It is of a good father to feed his children." Here certainly there is some word, such as "part" or "duty," left to be understood.

But the worst of these words that are understood is that they are not understood. Even in face of the few Latin precedents I rather doubt whether it is wise to follow such precedents, and certainly whether it is wise to create new precedents. But it is particularly undesirable at the present day, at a period in which things are emphatically not understood; a period in which they are, beyond all previous precedent, misunderstood. For men do not now agree, even as much as the Romans did, about the relations of a good man to the gods or the relation of a father to the children. At the best, there is some ambiguity in saying: "It is of a good man to go to church." For one man will read it in the form "It is the duty of a good man to go to church." Another may read it, in a cynical spirit, in the form "It is the interest of a good man to go to church." A third will read it in the form "It is the infernal bore inflicted on a good man to go to church." Now, that ambiguity did not so often happen in older and simpler social systems. There is less of that ambiguity in the Latin phrase. But there is nothing but ambiguity in the modern English phrase. There is only blank, unadulterated ambiguity in that English phrase —if you can call it an English phrase. And that is the root of my unrepentant revolt against it.

I mean that we may forgive the plumber (a form of Christian charity which many seem to find difficult) when he says that, in some small job, he has made good. But we only forgive him because we think that he, being poor and honest, really means "I have made good my word" or "I have made good my compact." But it is still true that a less honest plumber, and possibly a richer plumber, *might* mean by the phrase: "I have made good my intention to swindle this old fool," or "I have made good money out of this business, and much more than I had any right to receive."

Now, that is the moral ambiguity that I complain of, to start with, in the very nature of the phrase. But, in its actual modern use in any ordinary newspapers or novels, it goes far beyond ambiguity and becomes anarchy. It is bad policy, at the best, to allow a word to be understood; because it is first of all misunderstood, and afterwards mistaken or betrayed or supplanted by some baser word in the minds of baser people. Even if the man did originally mean: "I have made good my word," he will be unwise to leave out the word. It will be better, in every sense, if he keeps his word. A man's word is only too easy to forget. And, after a time, some meaner notion, such as making good his plan or plot or conspiracy, will have crept into the vacuum of that silence. But in the vulgar use of the phrase, in the modern world at this moment, there is not the remotest notion of anything so honest. Those who say that Hiram Q. Hogswash made good in Wall Street never did mean, and never were even supposed to mean, that he had made good any word or any contract or any honest purpose of any sort. Saying that Hiram made good simply means that Hiram made money, and never means anything else. Now, Hiram is not necessarily to be blamed for making money; but neither certainly is he to be praised for it. And this twisted and stunted form of words was invented so that he might be praised for it. By dragging in the word "good" where it is neither good grammar nor good ethics, a falsification of moral standards is created, tending to suggest that there is some connexion between making money and being good. So that, while we may invoke the ancient Roman to excuse the primary habit of leaving out logically necessary words, and while we may invoke the modern plumber ᐟto excuse the simpler sort of language about making good a job or a contract, we shall still lament over the larger and more desolating calamities that the Roman and the plumber, between them, have let loose upon the modern world. We shall recognize that this piece of phraseology is now, in fact, identified with a philosophy which teaches snobbish self-interest as a sort of ideal. If it is permissible to use a phrase like having made good, it is permissible to say that this particular phrase has most unmistakably made bad.

I DO not follow the fashions; I know little of that new wild world, where women can be wholly natural by constructing masks of grease-paint, or prove their freedom by strictly following the mode. I become conscious, or half-conscious, of some change in dress or deportment when it has already become general. In this manner, for instance, it was lately borne in upon me that another change has taken place in the human countenance.

It is already a commonplace, I suppose, that the ideal and immortal Lover, as conceived by Shakspere, "sighing like furnace, with a woeful ballad made to his mistress' eyebrow," must now go away and sigh about something else. His mistress has no eyebrows; and it might be inferred that he would produce no ballads. Anyhow, it suggests a sort of metaphysical duel between the Lover and the Poet, rather attractive to the metaphysical poets of that period. Would the balladist still cling to his ballad, pursuing the abstract and archetypal image of an Eyebrow, even when it was entirely detached from a face? Would he prefer the lady's eyebrow to the lady, leaving the rest of the lady behind like so much lumber, and pursuing only that peculiar vision of vanished hair? Or would he make the supreme sacrifice of tearing up the ballad and taking up with the lady, however strangely disfigured, resolving henceforward to write ballads only about her nose, her ears, or some portion of her which it seemed improbable that she would be in any immediate hurry to cut off? Even about those, of course, he could never be quite safe, if amputation were really the fashion.

In fact, touching that famous phrase, I have often wondered why modern poets do not more often amuse themselves by reproducing the imaginary Ballad to an Eyebrow. Shakspere is full of hints that could be used as the basis of all sorts of games and experiments; Browning accepted such a challenge in expanding the suggestive line of "Childe Roland to the Dark Tower came"; and my own father, who was a man of many crafts and hobbies he had no ambition to exploit, made a table ornament modelled in every detail on the Three Caskets of Portia. Surely some of us might have a shot at a really Elizabethan address to the supercilious feature. Surely any modern writer, after sighing like a furnace for a few minutes, might be able to attempt something appropriate in the sixteenth-century manner:

As seven-dyed Iris doth o'erarch the spheres,
Love made that bridge that doth o'erarch thine eyne
Bright as that bonded bow enskied; a sign
Against the crystal Deluge of thy tears
As line on line, so brow to brow appears . . .

At this point the poet looks up at the lady's eyebrow
and finds that it disappears. The pen drops from his
fingers, and this immortal fragment (if I may so
modestly describe it) remains for ever fragmentary.
Shakspere, especially the Shakspere of the Sonnets,
knew more than most people about the law of change
and dissolution spread over all earthly things, even
those that seem the most natural:

Since brass, nor stone, nor earth, nor boundless sea,
But sad mortality o'ersways their power,
How with this rage shall Beauty hold a plea,
Whose action is no stronger than a flower.

I quote from memory. Anyhow, even this argument does not force us to a premature plucking of the
flower or plucking out of the eyebrow. But, in spite
of Shakspere's somewhat excessive preoccupation, at
one period, with the images of mutability and mortality,

I very gravely doubt whether he ever did expect that sonnets or ballads to eyes, eyebrows, ears, noses, and the rest would ever become impossible by a general obliteration of these features. But what is stranger still, and what would have struck Shakspere as very strange indeed, is the fact that this negative and destructive operation should take place in a society devoted to pleasure, and in an age commonly supposed to be even more pagan than his own.

For the real moral is rather interesting. I challenge anybody to deny that this custom, if it had not been adopted as hedonism, would have been denounced as hideous asceticism. Suppose people had been told twenty years ago, say in the great Suffrage period, that in some ancient societies women were made to shave off their eyebrows after marriage. Would it not have been instantly classed with the cruel disfigurements imposed by masculine jealousy, as in the Oriental wives who are made to black their teeth after marriage? Suppose that some Puritan fanatic had indignantly declared that nuns were made to shave their eyebrows. Should we ever have heard the last of the unnatural deface-ment of the human face at the command of supersti-tion? Would not everybody have quite instinctively connected it with Fasts and Flagellants? Would it ever have occurred to anybody to connect it with fashion and pleasure? If anybody had told the Suffragette that the women in the harem liked having their hair pulled out an inch above their eyeballs, how the Suffragette would have yelled with derision of the cowardly masculine excuse! If anybody had told the late Mr. Kensit that a fashion of going bald above the eyes was started merely for fun among the nuns and novices themselves, how he would have snorted with incredulity! Yet the fashion has, to all appearance, been started merely for fun among the ladies themselves; and it may be presumed that they like it. I do not particularly care whether they have no eyebrows or three eyebrows, or green or triangular eyebrows, in those select circles where such things presumably start. But there is a certain intellectual interest in the way in which they seem nowadays, in so many cases, to start in the opposite direction from what one would normally call the pursuit of pleasure and beauty.

In short, the only real interest of such a trifle is that which connects it with some of the serious arts and decorative schools of our day. It is, I suppose, an unconscious expression, parallel to many other such expressions, of an artistic movement towards something that is more or less severe and harsh and even dehumanized. It is part of a tendency to turn people into patterns rather than into pictures. As a reaction against the deliquescent sentimentalism that was the end of the old humanitarian sentiment, it is comprehensible enough: but it is comprehensible rather than commendable.

Anyhow, one thing is certain; that, though many periods in the past have a certain grim and grandiose solemnity, through the hardness of externals or the mathematical severity of lines, these periods always appear to us to be oppressive and inhuman. So that the age of the Bright Young Things may yet have to look forward to its own appearance in history, as a type of tyranny and slavery and stiff as the mummies of the dead.

SOME time or other, I think, I will write a really thoughtful and educational article about Bed or Breakfast or Baths or Breathing, or some of those simple things, or things that seem simple to simple people. And it shall be written in the exact and peculiar style of a modern article on Marriage or the Family or Patriotism or Religion. I have read such multitudes of these modern articles, especially leading articles and articles in the lighter style of popular science; there are so many of them, and they are all so exactly alike, that I believe I could reproduce the manner pretty correctly and the type of argument, in so far as there is one. We will suppose, for the sake of argument, that I have selected the subject of "Food: Human Habit of Consuming." In which case I should be entirely safe, and even successful, if I wrote something like this:

"The progress of enlightenment, it must be admitted, tends to rob us of some of the emotional consolations which were possible to our ancestors in simpler times. Thinking men can no longer accept the ancient creeds and ecclesiastical dogmas which taught them that the virtues of an enemy whom they had eaten passed into their own bodies; the belief lingers in various forms in the common practice of eating beef and mutton, in the hope of thus absorbing the energy of the bull and the innocence of the sheep. And the modern Englishman, eating eggs and bacon at breakfast, hardly guesses that his real motive for doing so is a desire to partake mystically of the higher virtues of the pig or the bolder qualities of the chicken. It is not to be expected that these habits, resting as they do on such quaint survivals of savage superstition, should long survive the myths out of which they came; and the frequent appearance of Fasting Men at the World's Fair, in Barnum's Show, and other arenas of scientific experiment, is enough to show that science is again sending forth her pioneers to show humanity the better way. So long as the mediæval Church could impose her Feasts upon a faithful and obedient populace, the half-barbaric habit of having meals seemed almost to be a natural part of social life. There are many traces of the once-powerful tradition that bringing men together in love-feasts, or banquets of reconciliation, had a more or less magical effect of making them more friendly and more at peace with each other. And it may be that in ruder times even food itself was often useful for this psychological purpose, and was perhaps the only instrument that ignorant and primitive peoples could employ. Since the foundation of the League of Nations, men have learned the lesson that Peace Conferences can be successfully held without any of the old ceremonial gestures of eating or drinking, and any social use that such motions may once have served is now superseded by more direct and rational methods. The habit of eating may linger, here and there, among remote peasantries or rigid and reactionary individuals; but it is so clearly bound up with a whole world of ancient mystery and mummery, with the saying of grace, with the giving of thanks, with the proposing of patriotic sentiments over glasses of wine, that there can be little or no future for it now that man has reached his intellectual manhood. Gruncke, by the way, has pointed out that the cannibal notion of devouring and digesting the bodily vigour of an enemy is actually attested in the surviving popular phrase of 'drinking his health.' "

Now that is exactly like any number of newspaper and magazine articles I have read on the evolution of Marriage or Religion, only a little more sensible. The suggestion of Professor Gruncke about the anthropophagous meaning of drinking a health (though I have only just this moment made it up) is immeasurably more sensible than the suggestion of many professors on the subject of Marriage by Capture; proving that a bridegroom must be a brigand by the institution of the Best Man. They say solemnly that a chief always went out to the proposed abduction with some leading and distinguished man of his tribe. It never seems to dawn on them that he would have gone out in any case to any wedding, whether it were an abduction or not (or, indeed, to any occasion of any importance), with the leading men of his tribe. He would not be likely to select the most unpresentable and disreputable object in his tribe, when he went to visit his father-in-law. This ghastly and gaping lack of common sense, in all the attempted reconstructions of primitive human-ity, is the commonest mark of all this sort of popular science and fashionable rationalism. But it would be just as easy to use it to discredit Food as to discredit Family Life, or any of the basic human things that it is used to discredit. All that is necessary is to give a string of suggestions (such as I have just reeled off without stopping for breath) in the case of the Savage Custom of Supper. Mention a number of myths that have some connexion with meals; mix them all up like a soup; leave out all the joints and bones of argu-ment; and you can easily leave the reader with a general impression that a meal is a myth. Above all, you must keep on praising the reader, as a progressive fellow superior to his father; and you can easily make him feel superior to meals—until next meal-time.

There is no space here for my powerful and cogent exposure of the Superstition of Sleep. It is set forth (or it might be some day) with all the exact process of thought and careful citation of facts and scientific authorities essential to this sort of work; the footnotes fill up most of the pages and the appendices are in five volumes. The recognized scientific method in such cases consists of two parts. First the writer points out that Sleep has a perfectly simple, single, and obvious origin in mythology, and then (second) he proceeds to trace it to about ten totally contradictory mythological origins. In the epoch of the Sun Myth, he will say that sleep was a sort of negative worship of the Sun God. In order to emphasize the idea that men only lived by the life and inspiration of Apollo, the priests of Apollo (acting as mesmerists or medicine-men) succeeded in making their dupes literally lose consciousness after the sun's disappearance; induced them to die daily and lie like corpses until the dawn. That is quite a good one; but there will be plenty more. When poor old Herbert Spencer still had influence, it was often suggested that Dreams were the origin of Religion. To such thinkers, it would be a mere trifle to amend it by saying that Religion was the origin of Dreams. Sleep was only the hypnosis (how fortunate and illuminating

that the word hypnosis only means sleep!) imposed
by the priests on the credulous savages; in which state
all sorts of mythical suggestions could be made to them,
thus producing what we call the phenomena of dreams.
Therefore, as the world casts off priestly vestments and
pontifical mitres, it will also throw away bed-clothes,
night-gowns and nightcaps, and everything that reminds it of the mystical trance once called sleep. Or
it would be easy to show that sleep was produced among
primitive men by means of a vegetable drug (still used
in the Solomon Islands) that they might not spy on
the secret practices of the priests before they themselves had passed the Seventh Initiation. Or there is
the obvious explanation that the sacrifices demanded
at the harvest . . . but we need not go on with the
theories of the professors for ever, even if they do.

Perhaps you do not find this convincing. Perhaps
you do not propose instantly to abandon the habit of
eating or of sleeping at night. You say, defensively,
that food and sleep are necessary to normal men. I
fear it will be only too easy to apply the same argument to a belief in Free Will, to a concept of Right and
Wrong, and to the perilous habit of humanity of marry-
ing and having children.

DURING a brief but enforced leisure which has lately
befallen me I have read a great part of what was written
and spoken on the subject of Sir Walter Scott, during
the various celebrations of his Centenary. As a matter
of course, much of it was highly eulogistic, perhaps
rather too much as a matter of course. On the other
hand, a great part of it had a very unnecessary air of
apology, or a still more absurd air of patronage. Some
of it was flatly crude and uncomprehending. One
journalist not only announced jauntily that he could
see nothing in the literary legend or authority of Walter
Scott, but actually appealed against him to the authority
of Mark Twain. This affects me very much in the same
way as being told suddenly that Charlie Chaplin has
never got much pleasure out of Homer. I have no idea,
of course, of whether this is the case; Mr. Chaplin,
for all I know, may be a Homeric scholar and a deep
student of Scott; he may have better taste than Mark
Twain. Mark Twain was certainly something of a man
of genius in his own way; and so, for that matter, is
Charlie Chaplin. But there is such a thing as artistic

tradition and cultural grasp, and I should never have dreamed of expecting Mark Twain to understand the greatness of the Waverley Novels, any more than he understood the greatness of the Arthurian Romances. What he called The Yankee at the Court of King Arthur was, of course, a very clumsy version of King Arthur being tried in the court of the Yankee, and the findings of the court were about as conclusive as those of the court of Dayton, Tennessee.

Again, it may be true of Scott at the moment that he is neglected, upon a merely numerical estimate of readers; and the same, by this time, may very probably be true of Mark Twain. But that sort of calculation makes no difference to literary genius in the long run. There were also, of course, spirited defences; perhaps a little too much on the defensive. Mr. John Buchan stood resolutely with dirk and claymore before the shrine; but even in his excellent address one or two phrases suggested that he was not only defending a sanctity, but defending a secret. There was just a touch of that spirit with which the Scotsman sometimes seems to be almost forbidding the Englishman to understand Burns or to enjoy haggis. There is doubtless a truth in this tradition, for every writer who is really universal is also national; but Scott was not merely national, but very universal. Continental poets, like

Goethe and Victor Hugo, would hardly have been themselves without Scott. Byron, perhaps the most Continental of all poets, would not have been himself without Scott. Scott made Scottish Romances, but he made European Romance.

I think the two points about Scott that are the most vivid and vital are now the most invisible. They are points naturally neglected in our time, but the defect is in our time and not in Scott. One concerns the fact that he wrote historical novels, in the sense of stories full of historical characters. The other concerns the fact that he was himself a historical character. He really tells us much more about his own age than about the previous ages. It is too often forgotten that his best books, like *The Antiquary,* are actually about his own age. Some among the best are those very close to his own age, like *Rob Roy,* or the admirable ending of *Guy Mannering.* But there was something which Scott specially shared with his own epoch which he was always reading backwards into other epochs. It was not merely a vague thing that is called romance; it was also a very clear and classical thing that is called rhetoric. He was not an eighteenth-century man for nothing. He was, almost as much as he was anything, a great orator. It is one of the limitations of our own very limited time to sneer at oratory. But it is chiefly because our politicians cannot rise to it that our critics will not condescend to it. At the end of the eighteenth century there was a sort of glowing atmosphere of great speech, and in none more than in the men of action. Nelson and Napoleon were really as rhetorical as Danton and Fox.

Now, Scott possessed this sort of eloquence in the very highest degree. It would be well worth while to make an anthology of the mere speeches out of Scott's novels and metrical romances. From the retort of the Saxon Franklin upon De Bracy to the curse of Meg Merrilees upon the Laird of Ellangowan, from the speech with which the crabbed Louis XI rises into dignity in the face of death to the rude refusal of Douglas in Tantallon to give his hand to Marmion, all the speeches are spirited and telling, considered as speeches, whatever they may be considered as writings. This is much of the error about the rhymed romances. They are not always poetry, but they are always literature. They are literature of that particular kind that expresses itself in direct and militant oratory; in the speech that lies nearest to action. The reply of the Lady of Branksome, to the foes who hold her son as a hostage is almost doggerel considered as poetry; but it is direct and even deadly considered as oratory. Everything is apt and telling, from the sneer at Lord Dacre's courage to the abrupt turn of defiant invocation:

> For the young heir of Branksome's line
> God be his aid and God be mine.

That is the sort of way that men like Danton and
Fox did debate, through riots and revolutions that filled
Scott's own epoch. And he was more of a man of his
own epoch than he knew.

One thing he did find in the past, not yet quite
destroyed in the present, and it was his chief inspiration. He knew nothing of the religion of the past, and
his notion of Gothic was more barbarous than that of
any Goth. But he had extracted from his feudal traditions something on which his spirit truly fed; something without which the modern world is starving. He
found the idea of Honour, which is the true energy
in all militant eloquence. That a man should defend the
dignity of his family, of his farm, of his lawful rank
under the King, even of his mere name, of something
at least that was larger than himself—this was the fire
that Scott found still burning out of fourteenth-century
feudalism and expressed in eighteenth-century oratory.
Of all moral ideals it is the most neglected and misunderstood today. It is not strange that the eloquence
which sprang from it is misunderstood and neglected

also. We see that hollow gaping around us everywhere; in the fact that marriage is discussed as everything except what it is, a vow; or that property is discussed as everything except what it ought to be, an independence. But the modern world is not so happy in its oblivion of honour, or the eloquence that springs from honour, as to force us to believe in the permanent oblivion of Scott.

THE Sun has made a fitful and what may fairly be called a meteoric appearance in my garden this afternoon. And since, by a curious coincidence, this portent has occurred at a time not very distant from Midsummer Day (which, as you truly remark, is the Feast of St. John the Baptist and the date of the Battle of Bannockburn), the symbolical character of the sun flamed all the more mysteriously in the imagination. This luminary, which has been seldom observed of late in our country, can nevertheless be to a large extent calculated by astronomers, touching its actual though invisible relations to the earth. It would be an exaggeration to say that the sun visits England in the manner of a rare and very remote comet. It occurs in our literature; some say more often in our literature than our life, and I have even read a literary theory, according to which The Merry Month of May was a purely classical convention, taken wholesale by the English poets from the Provençal poets. So that Chaucer and Dunbar, huddled up in mackintoshes and cowering over stoves, wrote the praises of spring and summer with freezing fingers, and made purely ritual salutations to invisible flowers and impassable fields. I do not believe in this bitter interpretation, but then, I happen to be one of the few and rather unpopular persons who like the cool and troubled temper of the English climate. It was said that Germany wanted a place in the sun; I cannot sufficiently congratulate myself that England succeeded in finding a place in the shade. Not many people in England have agreed with me, this summer; though it is possible that I might find a few sympathizers in America, where there is a heat-wave. I remember once there was a heat-wave in England, and I found myself walking about on the Sussex Downs under that tropical oppression. And I remember that the rather hackneyed quotation from Browning came back to me; and I said with a groan: "Oh to be in April, now that England's here."

Anyhow, the sun has been made a symbol of all sorts of things, good, bad, and indifferent; and it would be easy to fill a page with all the significant parts it has played in human history; of what it meant to the Heretic Pharaoh and what to the Parsees; of why the rays of its rising are displayed on the blazon of Japan; of how it has been arrested by Joshua, worshipped by Julian, theorized about by Copernicus, quarrelled about by Galileo, pointed at by Napoleon, put in its proper place by Newton, and seriously disturbed and doubted about by Einstein—all this would give fascinating opportunity for that habit of wandering from the point which is the essence of an essay of this kind. For the moment, however, I prefer to regard the sun merely in the light of a strange star that has startled me by visiting my garden in the middle of summer, and rather to dwell upon the catastrophic and unearthly character of the event than to seek for any strictly scientific or merely rationalistic explanation of it.

One reason for reconciling oneself cheerfully to regarding the sun as a strange star is that it seems likely, in the light of the latest science, that we shall find it illuminating a very strange world. I am a child in these things; and so long as the child is allowed to play in the garden, he does not bother very much about the rules regulating the visits of that shining stranger, who has of late been very much of a stranger. But he does know enough about recent revolutions, in the ideas about space and light, and atomic structure, to know that not only the sun, but also the garden, grows more mysterious every day. We may come to regarding the sun almost as a secret; like the sun that wore the mask of the moon in Mr. Max Beerbohm's fairy-tale; a deceptive luminary; almost, if the contradiction be allowed, a dark luminary; with crooked rays; with invisible violet rays; with something resembling black rays, beyond the dreams of the blind. It seems to be anything but the simple golden globe with which the simple Victorian naturalists dealt so easily, when they taught us the use of the globes. Some of the things that are now said about it astonish me very much. For instance, Mr. René Fülop-Miller, the highly intelligent and impartial historian of the Bolshevist Revolution, has recently written a book about the Jesuits. The writer is equally detached about the Jesuits; he is entirely detached from the religion of the Jesuits. He is an ordinary modern rationalist; very emphatic upon the need to keep abreast of modern science. He narrates, as any rationalist would, as any reasonable man would, the victory of Galileo and the Copernican astronomy, with its earth going round the sun, over the old Ptolemaic astronomy, with its sun going round the earth. I should, of course, entirely accept that Copernican victory; it never would occur to me to do anything else. But I was considerably startled when Mr. Fülop-Miller, after stating the ordinary view of the Solar System, which everybody accepts, and I have naturally accepted, goes on calmly to write as follows:

"It is true that the most recent mathematical and physical theories necessitate a revision of this commonly held opinion, for no longer does the teaching of Ptolemy appear 'wholly false,' nor that of Copernicus 'alone true,' as Galileo thought. Rather does it appear that both the systems have fundamentally an equal claim to recognition, and that the superiority of the Copernican system rests solely on the greater simplicity of the astronomical calculations effected with its help. Cardinal Bellarmine had, however, already recognized this when he warned Galileo's pupils to regard the Copernican doctrine only as hypothetical and not as the sole truth."

In other words, the scientific rationalist, invoking the very latest scientific views, says something that I for one should never have dreamed of saying: that Galileo was as wrong as he was right; or at least that he was no more right than he was wrong, and no more right than his opponents were right. This seems to me a very amazing remark to appear in a book by an ordinary modern sceptic. Anyhow, it is a remark that will not be found in any book by me, or any of those who are regarded as religious reactionaries.

Let nobody go away and say that I made the remark. Let nobody wail aloud that I say the Solar System is a Solar Myth. I never interfered with the Solar System. I never disorganized the sun and moon;

I never in my life gave the planets or the fixed stars the least cause for uneasiness. Copernicus and Newton are good enough for me. I only say the sun must be a very strange star, and must stand in a very strange relation to a very strange planet or satellite, if any sane sceptic can really say that it is just as true that the sun goes round the earth as that the earth goes round the sun. The real truth, which he has in mind, is probably some very subtle mathematical relation, to which both of those contrary images are merely relative. The only effect on me, at the moment, is a merely imaginative, or even a merely artistic effect. It makes the sun much more extraordinary; and it was extraordinary enough before. I have not the faintest intention of meddling with these problems in the higher world of mathematics. I only say that the immediate effect of them on the fancy is almost to bring back the sun into the world of mythology. In that sense, the sun is much more of a Sun Myth; it is at least a Sun Mystery. Phoebus Apollo, worshipped with such superb prayer and sacrifice, is still at least like that other pagan god whom St. Paul saluted as the Unknown God. And because I love everything that adds at least to the wonder of the world, and because I hate familiarity as I hate contempt, I am glad that the strange god in the garden grows stranger every day. For we need mystery to console and encourage us. And, like Voltaire, and other pious and devout characters, I quite agree that we must cultivate the garden.

It is doubtless disrespectful to the reader, nor indeed does it tend greatly to the aggrandizement or dignity of the writer, to say that my occupation in life is catching flies. And when I recently referred to a certain type of Feminist as a wasp, I received remonstrances from one who doubtless considered her to have all the highest and most royal attributes of a queen bee. Nevertheless, this unfortunate metaphor frequently returns to my mind, and I am conscious of a truth that I could not easily express without it. What I mean is this: that one of the chief nuisances of our time is a swarm of little things, in the form of little thoughts, or little sayings largely divorced from thoughts, which pervade the whole atmosphere in a manner only comparable to that of the most minute insects: insignificant and almost invisible, but innumerable and almost omnipresent. I am not thinking of real thought; even of false or destructive thought. I am not referring to the real bodies of moral and philosophical opinion, based on principles I think wrong, or producing results I think mischievous. The views of this kind, with which I have sometimes dealt, differ very much in their power or promise or capacity for doing harm. I disagree with Communism as I disagree with Calvinism; but nobody would say this is the hour of Calvinism, and I admit, in a sense, it is the hour of Communism. There is a very strong intellectual temptation to the Bolshevist simplification because of the unquestionable collapse of the old commercial complexity. On the other hand, other theories I have quarrelled with in my time are less and less prominent in the modern quarrel. Many men of science have abandoned Darwinism. All men of science have abandoned Materialism. But Materialism and Darwinism were none the less thorough systems supported by thinking men, with arguments to be answered as well as assumptions to be questioned. The kind of thing of which I am speaking now is something at once atmospheric and microscopic, like a cloud of midges, and not like the serious scientific theories and philosophies of the nineteenth century, which may rather be compared, according to taste, to lions, elephants, tigers, vultures, vipers, or scorpions.

The matter in question is the prevalence of a sort of casual and even conversational scepticism, making even the idle thoughts of an idle fellow busy in the interests of doubt and despair. I mean that a man, without thinking at all, will throw off some flippant phrase which is always (by a strange fatality) a sort of feeble revolt against all traditional truth. It may be anything, an aside on the stage or a joke on the political platform; it may be a mere flourish at the start of a magazine story or a mere word dropped into an inconvenient silence; something said for the sake of saying something. The whole point of it is that it is, in this sense, pointless. The philosophy is not expressed when people are talking about philosophy, but when they are talking about anything else. I have just this moment started reading an ordinary modern story, quite well written considered as a story; and it begins by saying that there is not much difference between stupidity and courage, and, in fact, that courage is really only a form of stupidity.

That is exactly typical of the thing I mean. It is merely a casual remark; it is only very casually meant to be a clever remark; it is actually rather a silly remark; but the point is that a fatality of fashion causes a myriad such remarks to be made, always on the side of cowardice and never on the side of courage. In point of fact, of course, it would be easy to demonstrate its falsehood. History is full of examples of intellectual men who have been courageous, even of highly subtle and penetrating intellectuals who have accepted death courageously. It even contains any number of cases of thoughtful men who have thought a great deal about the act of accepting death; who have thought about it for a long time, and with complete composure, and then deliberately accepted it. Socrates is an obvious example. Sir Thomas More is a still more obvious example. Boëthius and many other philosophers; St. Paul and many other saints; all kinds of mystics, missionaries, religious founders and social reformers have proved the point over and over again. But I am interested here, not so much in the point, as in the pointless remark. What is that itch of intellectual irritation which makes a modern man, even in a moment of indolence, say the cynical thing even when it is obviously false; or kick against the heroic thing, even when it is self-evidently true? Why do we find today this vast and vague mass of trivialities, which have nothing in common except that they are *all* in reaction against the very best of human traditions? Why has this cheap and really worthless sort of scepticism got into such universal circulation? In other words, I am not now thinking of the Gold Standard of the highest truth, or the Bimetallism of the higher scepticism, which discusses whether there can be a rivalry in truth; or any of the more or less precious metals which may bear the image and superscription of this or that moral authority. I am puzzled by the circulation of all these millions of brass farthings, hardly more valuable than bad pennies; I am wondering where they all come from, and why they can be produced in such handfuls; and whether there is not something wrong with the mint of the mind. I am wondering what has debased the currency of current thought and speech, and why every normal ideal of man is now pelted with handfuls of such valueless pebbles, and assailed everywhere, not by free thought, but by frank thoughtlessness.

There seems to be no normal motive for a human being feeling a hostility to the human virtue of courage. He may disapprove of this or that excuse or occasion for calling it forth, but surely not of the thing itself. If the writer had said that the bravery of brave men is used by the stupidity of stupid men, he would have said something perfectly tenable, and, indeed, frequently true. When he says that a brave man must be a stupid man, he wantonly says something that can instantly be disproved and dismissed as impudent and idiotic. Why does he say it, except to relieve his feelings; and in that case what are his feelings? We only know that they have never yet been the normal feelings of men, yet they seem just now to be the almost involuntary feelings of a vast number of men. That is the problem that I find practically pestering us on every side today; and that is what I mean by comparing that buzz of dull flippancy to the swarming of gnats or flies. It is all concerned with the same paradox, with what may be called the omnipresence of the insignificant. A fly is a small thing, but flies can be a very big thing. In some tropical countries, I am told, they can appear like great clouds on the remote horizon or vast thunder-storms filling the whole sky. The plague of locusts which afflicts many lands is something much more destructive than the passage of a pack of wolves or the ruin wrought by a stampede of wild bulls or wild ele-phants. So the seemingly insignificant individual ir-ritation produced by these insignificant individual per-versities may be, in its cumulative effect, more corrupting to a whole culture than the great heresies that have been hardened and hammered into a certain intellectual solidity. The spirit of anarchy does not work only by monsters. Even the sages and visionaries of the East have seen a spiritual significance in the fact that even almost invisible insects can be a plague or carry a pesti-lence; and the ancient name of Beelzebub has the mean-ing of the Lord of Flies.